ALEXANDER
SOLZHENITSYN
SPEAKS
TO THE WEST

ALEXANDER SOLZHENITSYN SPEAKS TO THE WEST

THE BODLEY HEAD

LONDON SYDNEY

TORONTO

British Library Cataloguing
in Publication Data
Solzhenitsyn, Aleksandr Isaevich
Alexander Solzhenitsyn speaks to the West.
1. Civilization, Occidental
2. Communist strategy
I. Title
909'.09'9120827   CB245
ISBN 0-370-30175-7

Original Russian text copyright © 1975, 1978 by
Alexander Solzhenitsyn
Translation of the first three speeches by
Harris L. Coulter and Nataly Martin,
and edited for this edition by Alexis Klimoff
All rights reserved
Printed in Great Britain for
The Bodley Head Ltd
9 Bow Street London WC2E 7AL
by W & J Mackay Ltd, Chatham
Set in Monotype Garamond
First published in Great Britain 1978

CONTENTS

30 June 1975

Mr Solzhenitsyn delivered this speech in
Washington, DC, at a dinner which was
given in his honour by the American
Federation of Labor and Congress of
Industrial Organizations and hosted by
George Meany, the union's president.

Most of those present here today are workers.
Creative workers. And I myself, having spent
many years of my life as a bricklayer, as a foundry-
man, as a manual worker, in the name of all who
have shared this forced labour with me, like the
two Gulag prisoners whom you just saw,* and on
behalf of those who are doing forced labour in
our country, I can start my speech today with the
greeting: 'Brothers! Brothers in Labour!'

And not to forget the many honoured guests
present here tonight, let me add: 'Ladies and
gentlemen.'

'Workers of the world, unite!' Who of us has
not heard this slogan, which has been sounding
through the world for 125 years? Today you can
find it in any Soviet pamphlet as well as in every
issue of *Pravda*. But never have the leaders of the
Communist Revolution in the Soviet Union used
these words sincerely and in their full meaning.
When so many lies have accumulated over the
decades, we forget the radical and basic lie which

* Alexander Dolgun and Simas Kudirka.

is not on the leaves of the tree but at its very roots.

It is now almost impossible to remember or to believe . . . For instance, I recently reprinted a pamphlet from the year 1918. This was a detailed record of a meeting of all representatives of the factories in Petrograd, the city known in our country as the 'cradle of the Revolution'.

I repeat, this was March 1918, only four months after the October Revolution, and all the representatives of the Petrograd factories were denouncing the Communists who had deceived them in all their promises. What is more, not only had the Communists abandoned Petrograd to cold and hunger, themselves having fled from Petrograd to Moscow, but they had given orders to open machine-gun fire on the crowds of workers in the factory courtyards who were demanding the election of independent factory committees.

Let me remind you, this was March 1918. Scarcely anyone now can recall the other, similar acts: the crushing of the Petrograd strikes in 1921, the shooting of workers in Kolpino in the same year . . .

At the beginning of the Revolution, all those in the leadership, the Central Committee of the Communist Party, were *émigré* intellectuals who had returned after disturbances had already broken out in Russia to carry out the Communist Revolution. But one of them was a genuine worker, a highly skilled lathe operator until the last day of his life, Alexander Shliapnikov. Who is familiar with that name today? And yet it was he who expressed the true interests of the workers within the Communist leadership. In the years before the Revolution it was Shliapnikov who ran the whole

Communist Party in Russia – not Lenin, who was an *émigré*. In 1921, he headed the Workers' Opposition, which charged that the Communist leadership had betrayed the interests of the workers, that it was crushing and oppressing the proletariat and had degenerated into a bureaucracy.

Shliapnikov disappeared from sight. He was arrested later, and since he firmly stood his ground he was shot in prison; his name is perhaps unknown to most people here today. But I remind you: before the Revolution the head of the Communist Party of Russia was Shliapnikov – not Lenin.

Since that time, the working class has never been able to stand up for its rights and, in contrast to all the Western countries, our working class receives only handouts. It cannot defend its simplest, everyday interests, and the least strike for pay or for better living conditions is viewed as counter-revolutionary. Thanks to the closed nature of the Soviet system, you have probably never heard of the textile strikes in 1930 in Ivanovo, or of the 1961 worker unrest in Murom and Alexandrovo, or of the major workers' uprising in Novocherkassk in 1962 – this was in Khrushchev's time, well after the so-called thaw.

The story of this uprising will shortly be told in detail in my book, *The Gulag Archipelago*, III. It is a story of how workers went in peaceful demonstration to the Novocherkassk Party headquarters, carrying portraits of Lenin, to request a change in economic conditions. They were fired on with machine guns and dispersed with tanks. No family could even collect its wounded and dead: all were taken away in secret by the authorities.

I don't have to explain to those present here that in our country, ever since the Revolution, there has never been such a thing as a free trade union.

The leaders of the British trade unions are free to play the unworthy game of paying visits to imaginary Soviet trade unions and receiving odious visits in return. But the AFL-CIO has never given in to these illusions.

The American workers' movement has never allowed itself to be blinded and to mistake slavery for freedom. And today, on behalf of all of our oppressed people, I thank you for this!

In 1947, when liberal thinkers and wise men of the West, who had forgotten the meaning of the word 'liberty', were swearing that there were no concentration camps in the Soviet Union at all, the American Federation of Labor published a map of our concentration camps, and on behalf of all of the prisoners of those times, I want to thank the American workers' movement for this.

But just as we feel ourselves your allies here, there also exists another alliance – at first glance a strange and surprising one, but if you think about it, one which is well-founded and easy to understand: this is the alliance between our Communist leaders and your capitalists.

This alliance is not new. The very famous Armand Hammer, who flourishes here today, laid the basis for this when he made the first exploratory trip to Soviet Russia in Lenin's time, in the very first years of the Revolution. He was extremely successful in this reconnaissance mission and ever since then, for all these fifty years, we see continuous and steady support by the businessmen of the West for the Soviet Communist leaders. The clumsy and awkward Soviet economy, which could never cope with its difficulties on its own, is continually getting material and technological assistance. The major construction projects in the initial Five-Year Plan were built exclusively with American technology and materials. Even Stalin recognised that two thirds of what was needed was obtained from the West. And if today the Soviet Union has powerful military and police forces – in a country which is poor by contemporary standards – forces which are used to crush our movement for freedom in the Soviet Union – we have Western capital to thank for this as well.

Let me remind you of a recent incident which some of you may have read about in the newspapers, although others might have missed it: certain of your businessmen, on their own initiative, set up an exhibit of criminological technology in Moscow. This was the most recent and elaborate technology that here, in your country, is used to catch criminals, to bug them, to spy on them, to photograph them, to tail them, to identify them. It was all put on exhibit in Moscow in order that the Soviet KGB agents could study it, as if the businessmen did not understand what sort of criminals would be hunted down by the KGB.

The Soviet government was extremely interested in this technology and decided to purchase it. And your businessmen were quite willing to sell it. Only when a few sober voices here raised an uproar against it was this deal blocked. But you must realise how clever the KGB is. This technology didn't have to stay two or three weeks in a Soviet building under Soviet guard. Two or three nights were enough for the KGB to examine and copy it. And if today persons are being hunted down by the best and most advanced technology, for this I can also thank your Western capitalists.

This is something which is almost incomprehensible to the human mind: a burning greed for profit that goes beyond all reason, all self-control, all conscience, only to get money.

I must say that Lenin predicted this whole process. Lenin, who spent most of his life in the West and not in Russia, who knew the West much better than Russia, always wrote and said that the Western capitalists would do anything to strengthen the economy of the USSR. They will compete with each other to sell us cheaper goods and sell them quicker, so that the Soviets will buy from one rather than from the other. He said: 'They will bring us everything themselves without thinking about their future.' And, in a difficult moment, at a Party meeting in Moscow, he said: 'Comrades, don't panic, when things get very tough for us, we will give the bourgeoisie a rope, and the bourgeoisie will hang itself.'

Then Karl Radek, who was a very resourceful wit, said: 'Vladimir Ilyich, but where are we going to get enough rope to hang the whole bourgeoisie?'

Lenin effortlessly replied, 'They will sell it to us themselves.'

For decades on end, throughout the 1920s, the 1930s, the 1940s and 1950s, the Soviet press kept writing: Western capitalism, your end is near. We will destroy you.

But it was as if the capitalists had not heard, could not understand, could not believe this.

Nikita Khrushchev came here and said, 'We will bury you!' They didn't believe that either. They took it as a joke.

Now, of course, they have become more clever in our country. Today they don't say, 'We are going to bury you,' now they say, 'Détente.'

Nothing has changed in Communist ideology. The goals are the same as they were, but instead of the artless Khrushchev, who couldn't hold his tongue, now they say, 'Détente.'

In order to make this clear, I will take the liberty of presenting a short historic survey – the history of those relations which in different periods have been called 'trade', 'stabilisation of the situation', 'recognition of realities', and now 'détente'. These relations have at least a forty-year history.

Let me remind you with *what kind* of system relations began.

The system was installed by an armed uprising.

It dispersed the Constituent Assembly.

It capitulated to Germany – the common enemy.

It introduced punishment and execution without trial through the Cheka.

It crushed workers' strikes.

It plundered the countryside to such an unbelievable extent that the peasants revolted, and when this happened it crushed the peasants in the bloodiest possible manner.

It smashed the Church.

It reduced twenty provinces of our country to utter famine.

This was in 1921, the infamous Volga famine.

It was a typical Communist technique: to struggle for power without thinking of the fact that the productivity is collapsing, that the fields are not being sown, that the factories stand idle, that the country is sinking into poverty and famine – but when poverty and hunger do come, then to turn to the humanitarian world for help. We see this in North Vietnam today, Portugal is on the same path. And the same thing happened in Russia in 1921. When the three-year civil war, started by the Communists – and 'civil war' was a slogan of the Communists, civil war was Lenin's purpose; read Lenin, this was his aim and his slogan – when they had ruined Russia by civil war, then they asked America, 'America, feed our hungry.' And indeed, generous and magnanimous America did feed our hungry.

The so-called American Relief Administration was set up, headed by your future President Hoover, and indeed many millions of Russian lives were saved by this organisation of yours.

But what sort of gratitude did you receive for this? In the USSR not only did they try to erase this whole event from the popular memory – it's almost impossible in the Soviet press today to find any reference to the American Relief Administration – they even denounced it as a clever spy organisation, a cunning scheme of American imperialism to set up a spy network in Russia.

I continue: this was a system that introduced the first concentration camps in the history of the world.

This was a system that, in the twentieth century, was the first to introduce the use of hostages – that is to say, to seize not the person whom they were seeking, but rather a member of his family or simply someone at random, and to shoot him.

Such a system of hostages and the persecution of families exists to this day. It is still the most powerful weapon of persecution, because the bravest person, who is not afraid for himself, can flinch at a threat to his family.

This was a system which was the first – long before Hitler – to employ false announcements of registration, that is to say: 'Such and such persons must appear to register.' People would comply and then they were taken away to be killed. For technical reasons we didn't have gas chambers in those days. We used barges. A hundred or a thousand persons were put into a barge and then it was sunk.

This was a system which deceived the workers in all of its decrees – the decree on land, the decree on peace, the decree on factories, the decree on freedom of the press.

This was a system which exterminated all other parties. And let me make it clear to you that it not only disbanded each party, but destroyed its members. All members of every non-Communist party were exterminated.

This was a system which carried out genocide of the peasantry. Fifteen million peasants were shipped off to their deaths.

This was a system which introduced serfdom, the so-called passport system.

This was a system which, in time of peace, artificially created a famine, causing six million persons to die in the Ukraine between 1932 and 1933. They died on the very threshold of Europe.

And Europe didn't even notice it. The world didn't even notice it. Six million persons!

I could continue this enumeration, but I must stop because I have come to the year 1933 when, after all the facts I have named, your President Roosevelt and your Congress decided that this system was worthy of diplomatic recognition, of friendship, and of assistance.

Let me remind you that the great Washington did not agree to recognise the French Convention because of its savagery. Let me remind you that in 1933 voices were raised in your country objecting to recognition of the Soviet Union. However, this recognition took place and it was the beginning of friendship and ultimately of a military alliance.

Let us recall that in 1904 the American press was delighted at the Japanese victories and everyone wanted Russia's defeat because it was a conservative country. And in 1914 reproaches were directed at France and England for having entered into an alliance with such a conservative country as Russia.

The scope and the direction of my speech today do not permit me to say more about prerevolutionary Russia. I will only note that information about pre-revolutionary Russia was obtained by the West from persons who were either not sufficiently competent or not sufficiently scrupulous. I will cite for the sake of comparison some figures which you can read for yourself in *The Gulag Archipelago,* which has already been published in the United States, and perhaps many of you may have read it. Here are the figures:

According to the calculations of specialists,

based on the most precise and objective statistics, in the eighty years that preceded the Revolution in Russia – years of revolutionary activity with attempts on the Tsar's life, the assassination of a Tsar, revolutionary uprisings – during these years an average of seventeen persons a year were executed. The notorious Spanish Inquisition, during the decades when it was at the height of its murderous activity, executed perhaps ten persons a month. In *The Gulag Archipelago* I cite a book which was published by the Cheka in 1920, proudly reporting on its revolutionary achievements in 1918 and 1919 and apologising that its data was not quite complete: in 1918 and 1919 the Cheka executed, without trial, more than a thousand persons a month! This was written by the Cheka itself, before it understood how this would appear in historical perspective.

In 1937–8, at the height of Stalin's terror, if we divide the number of persons executed by the number of months, we get more than forty thousand persons shot per month! Here are the figures: seventeen a year, ten a month, more than one thousand a month, more than forty thousand a month! Thus, that which had made it difficult for the democratic West to form an alliance with pre-revolutionary Russia had, by 1941, grown to such an extent, yet still did not prevent the entire united democracies of the world – England, France, the United States, Canada, Australia, and other small countries – from entering into a military alliance with the Soviet Union. How is this to be explained? How can we understand it?

Here we can offer a few explanations. The first, I think, is that the entire united democracies of the world were too weak to fight against Hitler's Germany. If this is the case, then it is a terrible sign. It is a terrifying portent for the present day. If all these countries together could not defeat Hitler's little Germany, what are they going to do today, when more than half the globe is inundated by totalitarianism? I don't want to accept this explanation.

The second explanation is that perhaps there was simply panic among the statesmen of the day. They just didn't have sufficient confidence in themselves, they had no strength of spirit, and in this confused state they decided to enter into an alliance with Soviet totalitarianism. But this is also not flattering to the West.

Finally, the third explanation is that it was a deliberate choice. Democracy did not wish to defend itself. For defence it wanted to make use of another totalitarian system, the Soviet totalitarian system. I'm not talking now about the moral worth of such a choice, I'm going to talk about that later. But in terms of simple calculation, how shortsighted it is, what profound self-deception it demonstrates!

We have a Russian proverb: 'Don't call a wolf to help you against the dogs.' If dogs are attacking and tearing at you, fight against the dogs; do not call a wolf for help. Because when the wolves come, they will destroy the dogs or drive them away, but they will tear you apart as well.

World democracy could have defeated one totalitarian regime after another, the German, then the Soviet. Instead, it strengthened Soviet totalitarianism, consented to the birth of a third totalitarianism, that of China, and all this finally precipitated the present world situation.

Roosevelt, in Teheran, during one of his last toasts, said the following: 'I do not doubt that the three of us' – meaning Roosevelt, Churchill and Stalin – 'are leading our peoples in accordance with their desires and their aims.' How can this be understood? Let the historians worry about that. At the time, we listened and were astonished. We thought, 'When we reach Europe, we will meet the Americans, and we will tell them.' I was among the troops that were marching towards the Elbe. A little bit farther and I would have reached it and would have shaken the hands of your American soldiers. But just before that happened, I was taken off to prison and my meeting did not take place.

But now, after a great delay, the same hand has thrown me out of the country and here I am. After a delay of thirty years, my Elbe is here, today. I have come to tell you, as a friend of the United States, what, as friends, we wanted to tell you then, but what our soldiers were also prevented from telling you on the Elbe.

This is another Russian proverb: 'The yes-man is your enemy, but your friend will argue with you.' It is precisely because I am the friend of the United States, precisely because my speech is prompted by friendship, that I have come to tell you: 'My friends, I'm not going to give you sugary words. The situation in the world is not just dangerous, it isn't just threatening, it is catastrophic.'

Something that is incomprehensible to the ordinary human mind has taken place. In any case, the powerless, average Soviet people could not understand, year after year and decade after decade, what was happening. How were we to explain it? England, France, the United States, were the victors in World War II. Victorious states always dictate peace: they create the sort of situation which conforms to their philosophy, their concept of liberty, their concept of national interest. Instead of this, beginning in Yalta, your Western statesmen for some inexplicable reason signed one capitulation after another. Never did the West or your President Roosevelt impose any conditions on the Soviet Union for obtaining aid. He gave unlimited aid, and then unlimited concessions. Without any necessity whatever, the occupation of Mongolia, Moldavia, Estonia, Latvia, Lithuania was silently recognised in Yalta. After that, almost nothing was done to protect Eastern Europe, and seven or eight more countries were surrendered.

Stalin demanded that the Soviet citizens who did not want to return home be handed over to him, and the Western countries handed over 1.5 million human beings. How was this done? They were taken by force. English soldiers killed Russians who did not want to become prisoners of Stalin, and drove them by force to Stalin to be exterminated. This has recently come to light, just a few years ago. A million and a half human beings. How could the Western democracies have done this?

After that, for another thirty years, the constant retreat, the surrender of one country after another, to such a point that there are Soviet satellites even in Africa, almost all of Asia is taken over by them, Portugal is rolling down the precipice.

During those thirty years, more was surrendered to totalitarianism than any defeated country has ever surrendered after any war in history. There was no war, but there might as well have been.

For a long time we in the East couldn't understand this. We couldn't understand the flabbiness of the truce concluded in Vietnam. Any average Soviet citizen understood that this was a sly device which made it possible for North Vietnam to take over South Vietnam when it so chose. And then this arrangement was rewarded by the Nobel Prize for Peace – a tragic and ironic prize.

A very dangerous state of mind can arise as a result of these thirty years of retreat: give in as quickly as possible, give up as quickly as possible, peace and quiet at any cost.

This is what many Western papers wrote: 'Let's hurry up and end the bloodshed in Vietnam and have national unity.' (But at the Berlin Wall no one talks of national unity.) One of your leading newspapers, after the fall of Vietnam, had a full headline: THE BLESSED SILENCE. I would not wish that kind of 'blessed silence' on my worst enemy. I would not wish that kind of national unity on my worst enemy.

I spent eleven years in the Gulag Archipelago, and for half of my lifetime I have studied this question. Looking at this terrible tragedy in Vietnam from a distance, I can tell you that a million persons will simply be exterminated, while four to five million (in accordance with the scale of Vietnam) will find themselves in concentration camps and will be used to rebuild Vietnam. And you already know what is happening in Cambodia. It is a case of genocide. Full and complete destruction, only in a new form. Once again their technology is not up to building gas chambers. So, in a few hours, the entire capital city – the guilty capital city – is emptied out: old people, women, children are driven out without belongings, without food. 'Go and die!'

It is very dangerous for one's view of the world when this feeling comes on: 'Go ahead, give it up.' We already hear voices in your country and in the West: 'Give up Korea and let's live quietly.' Give up Portugal, of course; give up Japan, give up Israel, give up Taiwan, the Philippines, Malaysia, Thailand, give up ten more African countries. Just let us live in peace and quiet. Let us drive our big cars on our splendid highways; let us play tennis and golf unperturbed; let us mix our cocktails as we are accustomed to doing; let us see a beautiful smile and a glass of wine on every page of our magazines.

But look how things have turned out: in the West this has all turned into an accusation against the United States. We hear many voices saying, 'It's your fault, America.' I must today decisively defend the United States against these accusations.

I must say that the United States, of all the countries of the West, is the least guilty and has done most in order to prevent it. The United States has helped Europe to win the First and the Second World Wars. It twice raised Europe from postwar destruction – twice. For ten, twenty, thirty years it has stood as a shield protecting Europe while European countries counted their nickels to avoid paying for their armies (better yet, to have none at all), to avoid paying for armaments, thinking about how to leave NATO, knowing that in any case America will protect them. These countries started it all, despite their thousand-year-old civilisation and culture, even though they are closer to the danger and should have seen it more clearly.

I came to your continent; for two months I have been travelling in its wide-open spaces and I agree: here you must make an effort to understand the acuteness of the world situation. The United States has long shown itself to be the most magnanimous, the most generous country in the world. Wherever there is a flood, an earthquake, a fire, a natural disaster, an epidemic, who is the first to help? The United States. Who helps the most and unselfishly? The United States.

And what do we hear in reply? Reproaches, curses, 'Yankee Go Home'. American cultural centres are burned, and representatives from the Third World jump on tables to vote against the United States at the UN.

But none of this takes the load off America's shoulders. Whether you like it or not, the course of history has made you the leaders of the world. Your country can no longer think provincially. Your political leaders can no longer think only of their own states, of their own parties, of petty situations, which may or may not contribute to success at election time. You must think about the whole world. When a new political crisis arises (I believe we have just come to the end of a very acute crisis and the next one might come at any moment), the main decisions will fall inevitably on the shoulders of the United States.

In my stay here, I have heard some explanations

of the situation. Let me quote some of them: 'It is impossible to protect those who do not have the will to defend themselves.' I agree with that, but this was said about South Vietnam. Yet in one half of today's Europe and in three quarters of today's world the will for self-defence is even less than it was in South Vietnam.

We are told: 'We cannot defend those who are unable to defend themselves with their own human resources.' But against the overwhelming forces of totalitarianism, when all of this power is thrown against a country – no country can defend itself with its own resources. For instance, Japan doesn't have a standing army.

We are told: 'We should not protect those who do not have a full democracy.' This is the most remarkable argument of all. This is the leitmotif I hear in your newspapers and in the speeches of some of your political leaders. Who in the world, when on the front line of defence against totalitarianism, has ever been able to sustain a full democracy? You, the united democracies of the world, were not able to sustain it. America, England, France, Canada, Australia together did not sustain it. At the first threat of Hitlerism, you stretched out your hands to Stalin. You call that sustaining democracy? Hardly.

And there are other arguments (there have been a great many such speeches): 'If the Soviet Union is going to use détente for its own ends, then we . . .' But what will happen then? The Soviet Union has used détente, is using it now, and will continue to use it in its own interests! For example, China and the Soviet Union, both actively participating in détente, have quietly grabbed three countries of Indochina. True, perhaps as a consolation, China will send you a ping-pong team. Just as the Soviet Union once sent you the pilots who crossed the North Pole. And in a few days there will be the flight into space together.

A typically well-staged diversion. I remember very well the time, June 1937, when Chkalov, Baidukov, and Belyakov heroically flew over the North Pole and landed in the state of Washington. This was the very year when Stalin was executing more than forty thousand persons a month. And Stalin knew what he was doing. He sent those pilots and aroused in you a naïve delight – the friendship of two countries across the North Pole. The pilots were heroes, nobody will deny them that. But this was a show to divert you from the real events of 1937. And what is the occasion now? Could it be an anniversary of that flight thirty-eight years ago? Is thirty-eight years some kind of an anniversary? No, it is simply necessary to cover up Vietnam. Once again, those pilots were sent here. The Chkalov Memorial was unveiled in the state of Washington. Chkalov was a hero and is worthy of a memorial. But to present the true picture, there should have been a wall behind the memorial and on it there should have been a bas-relief showing the executions, showing the skulls and skeletons.

We are also told (I apologise for so many quotes, but there are many more in your press and radio): 'We cannot ignore the fact that North Vietnam and the Khmer Rouge have violated the agreement, but we're ready to look to the future.' What does this mean? It means: let them exterminate people. If these murderers, who live by violence, these executioners, offer us détente, we will be happy to go along with them. As Willy Brandt once said: 'I would even be willing to have détente with Stalin.' At a time when Stalin was executing forty thousand a month he would have been willing to have détente with Stalin?

Look into the future! This is how they looked into the future in 1933 and 1941, but it was a shortsighted look. This is how they looked into the future two years ago when a senseless, incomprehensible, non-guaranteed truce in Vietnam was negotiated. Once again it was a shortsighted view. There was such a hurry to make this truce that they forgot to liberate your own Americans from captivity. They were in such a hurry to sign this document that some three thousand Americans were left there: 'Well, they vanished; we can get by without them.' How was this done? How can this be? Part of them, indeed, may be missing in action, but the leaders of North Vietnam themselves have admitted that some of them are still being kept in prison. And do they return your countrymen? No, instead of returning them, they keep laying down new conditions. At first they said, 'Remove Thieu from power.' Now they say, 'Let the United States restore a unified Vietnam, otherwise it's very difficult to find these people.'

If the government of North Vietnam has difficulty explaining to you what happened to your brothers, your American POWs who have not yet returned, I can explain this quite clearly on the basis of my experience in the Gulag

Archipelago. There is a law in the Archipelago that those who have been treated the most harshly and who have withstood the most bravely, who are the most honest, the most courageous, the most unbending, never again come out into the world. They are never again shown to the world because they will tell tales that the human mind can barely accept. Some of your returned POWs told you that they were tortured. This means that those who have remained were tortured even more, but did not yield an inch. These are your best people. These are your foremost heroes, who, in a solitary combat, have stood the test. And today, unfortunately, they cannot take courage from our applause. They can't hear it from their solitary cells where they may either die or remain for thirty years like Raoul Wallenberg, the Swedish diplomat who was seized in 1945 in the Soviet Union. He has been imprisoned for thirty years and they will not give him up.

And yet you had some hysterical public figures who said: 'I will go to North Vietnam. I will get on my knees and beg them to release our prisoners of war.' This is no longer a political act – this is masochism.

To make you understand properly what détente has meant in these forty years – friendship, stabilisation of the situation, trade, etc – I must tell you something which you have not seen or heard: how it looked from the other side. Let me give you some examples. Mere acquaintance with an American, and God forbid that you should sit with him in a café or restaurant, meant a ten-year term for suspicion of espionage.

In the first volume of *The Gulag Archipelago* I

tell of an event which was recounted not by some insignificant arrested person but by all of the members of the Supreme Court of the USSR during that brief period when I was in the good graces of the regime under Khrushchev. A Soviet citizen had been in the United States and on his return said that they have wonderful roads there. The KGB arrested him and demanded a term of ten years, but the judge said: 'I don't object, but there is not enough evidence. Couldn't you find something else against him?' So the judge was exiled to Sakhalin because he dared to argue, and they gave the other man ten years. Just imagine what 'lie' he had told! And what 'praise' this was of American imperialism: in America there are good roads! Ten years.

In 1945–6 many persons passed through our prison cells. They had not co-operated with Hitler, although there were some of those too. As a rule they were not guilty of anything, but simply had been in the West and had been liberated from German prison camps by the Americans. This was considered a criminal act: liberated by the Americans. It meant he has seen the good life. If he comes back he will talk about it. The most terrible thing is not what he did but what he would talk about. And all such persons got ten-year terms.

During Nixon's last visit to Moscow your American correspondents gave their reports from the streets of Moscow: Here I am, going down a Russian street with a microphone and asking ordinary Soviet citizens: 'Tell me, please, what do you think of the meeting between Nixon and Brezhnev?' And, amazingly, every last per

(28)

son answered: 'Wonderful. I'm delighted. I'm absolutely overjoyed!'

What does this mean? If I'm going down a street in Moscow and some American comes up to me with a microphone and asks me something, then I know for certain that a member of the state security is close by, also with a microphone, and is recording everything I say. Do you think that I'm going to say something that is going to put me in prison immediately? Of course I say, 'It's wonderful, I'm overjoyed.'

But what is the worth of such correspondents if they simply transfer Western methods over there without thinking things through?

For many years you helped us with Lend-Lease, but we've now done everything to forget this, to erase it from our minds, not to recall it if at all possible. Before I came here, I delayed my visit to Washington a little in order to take a look at some ordinary parts of America, to visit several states and simply to talk with people. I was told, and I learned this for the first time, that in every state during the war years there were Soviet-American friendship societies which collected assistance for the Soviet people – warm clothes, canned food, gifts – and sent them to the Soviet Union. Not only did we never see these things or receive them (they were distributed somewhere among the privileged circles), but no one even told us that this was being done. I only learned about it for the first time here, this month, in the United States.

Everything poisonous which could be said about the United States was said in Stalin's day. And all of this is a heavy sediment which can be stirred up at any time. Any day the newspapers can come out with the headline BLOODTHIRSTY AMERICAN IMPERIALISM WANTS TO SEIZE CONTROL OF THE WORLD, and this poison will rise up again and many people in our country will believe and will consider you aggressors. This is how détente has been managed on our side.

The Soviet system is so closed that it is almost impossible for you to understand it from here. Your theoreticians and scholars write monographs, they try to understand and explain what is taking place there. Here are some of these naïve explanations, which cannot fail to amuse us Soviet people. It is said, for example, that the Soviet leaders have now given up their inhumane ideology. Not at all. They haven't given it up one bit. Others say that in the Kremlin there are some on the left, some on the right; they are fighting with each other, and we have to behave in such a way so that we don't interfere with those on the left. This is all fantasy: left, right. There is some sort of a struggle for power, of course, but they all agree on the essentials.

There also exists the following theory: that now, thanks to the growth of technology, there is a technocracy in the Soviet Union, a growing number of engineers, and the engineers are now running the economy and they, not the Party, will soon determine the fate of the country. But I will tell you that the engineers will determine the fate of the country just as much as our generals will determine the fate of the army. That means zero. Everything is done the way the Party demands. That is our system. Judge it for yourself.

It is a system where for forty years there have

not been genuine elections, but simply a comedy, a farce. Thus, a system which has no legislative machinery. It is a system without an independent press; a system without an independent judiciary; where the people have no influence either on external or internal policy; where any thought which is different from the state's is crushed.

And let me tell you that electronic bugging in our country is such a simple thing that it is a matter of everyday life. You had an incident in the United States where a bugging caused an uproar which lasted for a year and a half. For us it's an everyday matter. Almost every apartment, every institution has its bug, and it doesn't surprise us in the least – we are used to it.

It is a system where unmasked butchers of millions, like Molotov and some lesser men, have never been tried in the courts but retire on enormous pensions in the greatest comfort. It is a system where the show still goes on today and where every foreigner who wants to see the country is surrounded by several planted agents working according to a fixed scenario. It is a system where the constitution has never been adhered to for one single day; where all the decisions are reached in secrecy, among a small, irresponsible clique, and are then flung down on us and on you like a bolt of lightning.

And what are the signatures of these people worth? How could one rely on their signatures in the documents of détente? You might ask your specialists now and they'll tell you that in recent years the Soviet Union has succeeded in achieving superiority in chemical weapons and in missiles over the United States.

So what are we to conclude from that? Is détente needed or not? Not only is it needed, it is as necessary as air. It is the only way of saving the earth – instead of a world war to create détente, a true détente, and if it has already been ruined by the bad word which we use for it – 'détente' – then we should find another word.

I would say that there are very few, only three, main characteristics of such a true détente.

In the first place, there would be disarmament – but a dismantling of the weapons of war as well as those of violence. We must stop using not only the kind of arms that are used to destroy one's neighbours but also the kind that are used to oppress one's fellow countrymen. It is hardly détente if we here can spend our time agreeably, while over there people are groaning and dying or confined in psychiatric hospitals. Doctors are making their evening rounds, injecting people with the third daily dose of drugs which destroy the brain.

The second sign of true détente, I would say, is the following: that it should not be based on smiles, not on verbal concessions but on a firm foundation. You know the words from the Bible: build not on sand, but on rock. There has to be a guarantee that détente will not be violated over-night. For this the other party to the agreement must have its acts subject to control by public opinion, by the press, and by a freely elected parliament. And until such control exists there is absolutely no guarantee.

There is a third simple condition. What kind of détente is it when they employ the sort of malevolent propaganda which is proudly called 'ideological warfare' in the Soviet Union? Let us not have that. If we're going to be friends, let's be friends; if we're going to have détente, then let's have détente, and an end to ideological warfare.

The Soviet Union and the Communist countries know how to conduct negotiations. For a long time they make no concessions and then they give in just a little bit. Right away there is rejoicing: 'Look, they've made a concession; it's time to sign.' For two years the European negotiators of thirty-five countries have painfully been negotiating and their nerves have been stretched to the breaking point; finally they gave in. A few women from the Communist countries may now marry foreigners. A few newspapermen will now be permitted to travel a little more than before. They give one one-thousandth of what natural law should provide – things which people should be able to do even before such negotiations are undertaken – and already there is joy. And here in the West we hear many voices that say: 'Look, they're making concessions; it's time to sign.'

During these two years of negotiations, in all the countries of Eastern Europe, even in Yugoslavia and Romania, the pressure has increased, the oppression intensified. And it is precisely now that the Austrian chancellor says, 'We must sign this agreement as rapidly as possible.'

What sort of an agreement will this be? The proposed agreement is the funeral of Eastern Europe. It means that Western Europe will finally, once and for all, sign away Eastern Europe, stating that it is perfectly willing to see

Eastern Europe oppressed, only please don't bother us. And the Austrian chancellor thinks that if all these countries are pushed into a mass grave, Austria, at the very edge, will somehow survive and not fall into it as well.

And we, from the whole of our life experience there, have concluded that there is only one way to withstand violence: with firmness.

You have to understand the nature of Communism. The very ideology of Communism, all of Lenin's teachings, are that anyone who doesn't take what's lying in front of him is considered a fool. If you can take it, do so. If you can attack, strike. But if there's a wall, then retreat. The Communist leaders respect only firmness and have contempt for persons who continually give in to them. Your people are now saying – and this is the last quotation I am going to give you from the statements of your leaders – 'Power, without any attempt at conciliation, will lead to a world conflict.' But I would say that power with continual acquiescence is not power at all.

From our experience I can tell you that only firmness makes it possible to withstand the assaults of Communist totalitarianism. History offers many examples, and let me give you some of them. Look at little Finland in 1939, which by its own forces withstood the attack. You, in 1948, defended Berlin only by your firmness of spirit, and there was no world conflict. In Korea in 1950 you stood up to the Communists, only by your firmness, and there was no world conflict. In 1962 you forced the missiles to be removed from Cuba. Again it was only firmness, and there was no world conflict. The late Konrad Adenauer conducted firm negotiations with Khrushchev and initiated a genuine détente with Khrushchev, who started to make concessions. If he hadn't been removed, he would have gone to Germany that winter to continue the genuine détente.

Let me remind you of the weakness of a man whose name is rarely associated with weakness – Lenin. When he came to power, Lenin, panic-stricken, gave up to Germany everything Germany demanded. Whatever they asked for. Germany took as much as it wanted and said, 'Give Armenia to Turkey.' And Lenin said, 'Fine.' It's almost an unknown fact that Lenin petitioned the Kaiser to act as intermediary to persuade the Ukraine to settle a boundary between the Communists and the Ukraine. It wasn't a question of seizing the Ukraine but only of creating this boundary.

We, the dissidents of the USSR, have no tanks, no weapons, no organisation. We have nothing. Our hands are empty. We have only our hearts and what we have lived through in the half century under this system. And whenever we have found the firmness within ourselves to stand up for our rights, we have done so. It is only by firmness of spirit that we have withstood. And if I am standing here before you, it is not because of the kindness or the good will of Communism, not thanks to détente, but due to my own firmness and your firm support. They knew that I would not yield an inch, not a hair's breadth. And when they could do nothing they themselves fell back.

This is not easy. We learned from the difficulties of our own life. And if you yourselves – any one of you – were in the same difficult situation, you would have learned the same thing. Take Vladimir Bukovsky, whose name is now almost forgotten. I don't want to enumerate a lot of names because however many I might mention there are still more, and when we resolve the question with two or three names it is as if we forget and betray the others. Instead, we should remember figures: there are tens of thousands of political prisoners in our country and – by the calculation of British specialists – seven thousand persons are now under compulsory psychiatric treatment. For example, Vladimir Bukovsky. It was proposed to him, 'All right, we'll free you. Go to the West and shut up.' And this young man, a youth now on the verge of death, said: 'No, I won't go under those conditions. I have written about the persons you have put in insane asylums. You release them and then I'll go to the West.' This is what I mean by that firmness of spirit to stand up against granite and tanks.

Finally, to evaluate everything that I have said to you, we need not remain on the level of practical calculations. Why did such and such a country act in such and such a way? What were they counting on? Instead, we should rise above this to the moral level and say: 'In 1933 and in 1941 your leaders and the whole Western world made an unprincipled deal with totalitarianism.' We will have to pay for this; some day it will come back to haunt us. For thirty years we have been paying for it. And we're going to pay for it in an even worse way in the future.

One cannot think only on the low level of political calculations. It is also necessary to think of what is noble, and what is honourable – not just of what is profitable. Resourceful Western legal scholars have now introduced the term 'legal realism', which they can use to obscure any moral evaluation of affairs. They say, 'Recognise realities: if certain laws have been established in countries ruled by violence, these laws still must be recognised and respected.'

At the present time it is widely accepted among lawyers that law is higher than morality – law is something which is shaped and developed, whereas morality is something inchoate and amorphous. This is not the case. The opposite is true: morality is higher than law! Law is our human attempt to embody in rules a part of that moral sphere which is above us. We try to understand this morality, bring it down to earth, and present it in the form of law. Sometimes we are more successful, sometimes less. Sometimes we have a mere caricature of morality, but morality is always higher than law. This view must never be abandoned. We must acknowledge it with our hearts and souls.

In the twentieth century it is almost a joke in the Western world to use words like 'good' and 'evil'. They have become old-fashioned concepts, yet they are very real and genuine. These are concepts from a sphere which is above us. And instead of getting involved in base, petty, shortsighted political calculations and games we must recognise that a concentration of evil and a tremendous force of hatred is spreading throughout the world. We must stand up against it and not hasten to give, give, give everything that it wants to swallow.

Today there are two major trends in the world.

The first is the one I have just described to you, which has been going on for more than thirty years. It is a process of shortsighted concessions; a process of giving up and giving up and giving up in the hope that perhaps at some point the wolf will have eaten enough.

The second trend is one which I consider the key to everything and which, I predict, will bring all of us our future. Under the cast-iron shell of Communism – for twenty years in the Soviet Union and for a shorter time in other Communist countries – a liberation of the human spirit is occurring. New generations are growing up, steadfast in their struggle with evil, unwilling to accept unprincipled compromises, preferring to lose everything – salary, living conditions, life itself – so as not to sacrifice conscience, unwilling to make deals with evil.

This trend has gone so far that, in the Soviet Union today, Marxism has fallen to such a low point that it has become a joke, an object of contempt. No serious person in our country today, not even university and high-school students, can talk about Marxism without a smile or a sneer. But this process of our liberation, which obviously will entail social transformations, is slower than the first one – the process of concessions. Over there, when we see these concessions we cannot understand. Why so quickly? Why so precipitate? Why yield several countries in one year?

I started by saying that you are the allies of our liberation movement in the Communist countries. I call upon you: let us think together and try to see how we can adjust the relationship between these two trends. Whenever you help the persons persecuted in the Soviet Union, you not only display magnanimity and nobility, you are not only defending them, but yourselves as well. You are defending your own future.

So let us try and see how far we can go to stop this senseless and immoral process of endless concessions to the aggressor, these slick legal arguments for giving up one country after another. Why must we hand over to Communist totalitarianism more and more technology – complex, sophisticated technology which it needs for armaments and for oppressing its own citizens? If we can at least slow down that process of concession, if not stop it altogether, and make it possible for the process of liberation to continue in the Communist countries, then ultimately these two processes will yield us our future.

On our crowded planet there are no longer any 'internal affairs'. The Communist leaders say, 'Don't interfere in our internal affairs. Let us strangle our citizens in peace and quiet.' But I tell you: interfere more and more. Interfere as much as you can. We beg you to come and interfere.

Understanding my own task in the same way, I have perhaps interfered today in your internal affairs, or at least touched upon them, and I apologise for it.

I have travelled around the United States and this has been added to my earlier understanding of it – what I have heard from listening to the radio, from talking to men of experience.

For me and my friends, for people who think the way I do over there, for all ordinary Soviet citizens, America evokes a mixture of admiration and compassion. Admiration for your own tremendous forces which perhaps you don't even recognise yourselves. You're a country of the future, a young country, with yet untapped possibilities, enormous territory, great breadth of spirit, generosity, magnanimity. But these qualities – strength, generosity, and magnanimity – are usually combined in a man and even in a whole country with trustfulness. And this has already done you a disservice several times.

I would like to call upon America to be more careful with its trust to prevent these pundits who are attempting to establish fine degrees of justice and even finer legal shades of equality (some because of their distorted outlook, others because of shortsightedness, still others out of self-interest), to prevent them from using the struggle for peace and for social justice to lead you down a false road. They are trying to weaken you; they are trying to disarm your strong and magnificent country in the face of this fearful threat – one which has never before been seen in the history of the world. Not only in the history of your country, but in the history of the world.

I call upon you: ordinary working men of America, represented here by your trade union movement, do not let yourselves become weak. Do not let yourselves be led in the wrong direction. Let us try to slow down the process of concessions and help the process of liberation!

9 July 1975

Mr Solzhenitsyn delivered this speech in New York at a luncheon which was given in his honour by the American Federation of Labor and Congress of Industrial Organizations and hosted by Lane Kirkland, the union's secretary-treasurer.

Is it possible or impossible to transmit the experience of those who have suffered to those who have yet to suffer? Can one part of humanity learn from the bitter experience of another or can it not? Is it possible or impossible to warn someone of danger?

How many witnesses have been sent to the West in the last sixty years? How many waves of immigrants? How many millions of persons? They are all here. You meet them every day. You know who they are: if not by their spiritual disorientation, their grief, their melancholy, then you can distinguish them by their accents or their external appearance. Coming from different countries, without consulting with one another, they have brought out exactly the same experience; they tell you exactly the same thing: they warn you of what is now taking place and of what has taken place in the past. But the proud skyscrapers stand on, jut into the sky, and say: 'It will never happen here. This will never come to us. It is not possible here.'

It can happen. It is possible. As a Russian proverb says: 'When it happens to you, you'll know it's true.'

But do we really have to wait for the moment when the knife is at our throat? Couldn't it be possible, ahead of time, to assess soberly the world-wide menace that threatens to swallow the whole world? I was swallowed myself. I have been in the dragon's belly, in its red-hot innards. It was unable to digest me and threw me up. I have come to you as a witness to what it is like there, in the dragon's belly.

It is astonishing that Communism has been writing about itself in the most open way, in black and white, for 125 years, and even more openly, more candidly in the beginning. The *Communist Manifesto*, for instance, which everyone knows by name, and which almost no one ever takes the trouble to read, contains even more terrible things than what has actually been done. It is perfectly amazing. The whole world can read, everyone is literate, yet somehow no one wants to understand. Humanity acts as if it does not understand what Communism is, as if it does not want to understand, is not capable of understanding.

I think it is not only a question of the disguises that Communism has assumed in the last decades. It is rather that the essence of Communism is quite beyond the limits of human understanding. It is hard to believe that people could actually plan such things and carry them out. And it is precisely because its essence is beyond comprehension, perhaps, that Communism is so difficult to understand.

In my last address in Washington I spoke a

great deal about the Soviet state system, how it was created and what it is today. But it is perhaps more important to discuss with you the ideology that inspired the system, created it, and still governs it. It is much more important to understand the essence, and above all the legacy, of this ideology which has not changed at all in 125 years. It has not changed since the day it was created.

That Marxism is not a science is entirely clear to intelligent people in the Soviet Union. One would even feel awkward to refer to it as a science. Leaving aside the exact sciences, such as physics, mathematics, and the natural sciences, even the social sciences can predict an event – when, in what way, and how an event might occur. Communism has never made any such forecasts. It has never said where, when, and precisely what is going to happen. Nothing but declamations. Rhetoric to the effect that the world proletariat will overthrow the world bourgeoisie and the most happy and radiant society will then arise. The fantasies of Marx, Engels, and Lenin break off at this point, not one of them goes any further to describe what this society would be like. They simply say: the most radiant, most happy society. Everything for the sake of man.

I wouldn't want to enumerate for you all the unsuccessful predictions of Marxism, but I can give you a few. For example, it was claimed that the conditions of the working class in the West would deteriorate steadily, get more and more unbearable, until the workers would be reduced to total poverty. (If only in our country we could feed and clothe our working class, provide it with everything, and give it as much leisure as you do!)

Or the famous prediction that Communist revolutions would begin in such advanced industrial countries as England, France, America, Germany. (But it worked out exactly the other way, as you know.) Or the prediction that socialist states would not even exist. As soon as capitalism was overthrown, the state would at once wither away. (Look about you: where can you see states as powerful as in the so-called socialist or Communist countries?) Or the prediction that wars are inherent only to capitalism; as soon as Communism is introduced, all wars will come to an end. (We have also seen enough of this: in Budapest, in Prague, on the Soviet-Chinese border, in the occupation of the Baltic countries, and when Poland was stabbed in the back. We have seen enough of this already, and we will surely see more yet.)

Communism is as crude an attempt to explain society and the individual as if a surgeon were to perform his delicate operations with a meat axe. All that is subtle in human pyschology and in the structure of society (which is even more complex), all of this is reduced to crude economic processes. This whole created being – man – is reduced to matter. It is characteristic that Communism is so devoid of arguments that it has none to advance against its opponents in our Communist countries. It lacks arguments and hence there is the club, the prison, the concentration camp, and insane asylums with forced confinement.

Marxism has always opposed freedom. I will quote just a few words from the founding fathers of Communism, Marx and Engels (I quote from the first Soviet edition of 1929): 'Reforms are a sign of weakness' (vol. 23, p. 339); 'Democracy is more to be feared than monarchy and aristocracy' (vol. 2, p. 369); 'Political liberty is a false liberty, worse than the most abject slavery' (vol. 2, p. 394). In their correspondence Marx and Engels frequently stated that terror would be indispensable after achieving power, that 'it will be necessary to repeat the year 1793. After achieving power, we'll be considered monsters, but we couldn't care less' (vol. 25, p. 187).

Communism has never concealed the fact that it rejects all absolute concepts of morality. It scoffs at any consideration of 'good' and 'evil' as indisputable categories. Communism considers morality to be relative, to be a class matter. Depending upon circumstances and the political situation, any act, including murder, even the killing of hundreds of thousands, could be good or could be bad. It all depends upon class ideology. And who defines this ideology? The whole class cannot get together to pass judgment. A handful of people determine what is good and what is bad. But I must say that in this very respect Communism has been most successful. It has infected the whole world with the belief in the relativity of good and evil. Today, many people apart from the Communists are carried away by this idea. Among progressive people, it is considered rather awkward to use seriously such words as 'good' and 'evil'. Communism has managed to persuade all of us that these concepts are old-fashioned and laughable. But if we are to be deprived of the concepts of good and evil, what will be left? Nothing but the manipulation of one another. We will sink to the status of animals.

Both the theory and the practice of Communism are completely inhuman for that reason. There is a word very commonly used these days: 'anti-Communism'. That is a poor, tasteless locution. It makes it appear as though Communism were something original, fundamental. Therefore, it is taken as the point of departure, and anti-Communism is defined in relation to Communism. I say that this word was poorly selected, that it was put together by people who do not understand etymology. The primary, the eternal concept is humanity, and Communism is anti-humanity. Whoever says 'anti-Communism' is saying, in effect, anti-anti-humanity. A poor construction. So we should say: that which is against Communism is for humanity. Not to accept, but to reject this inhuman Communist ideology is simply to be a human being. Such a rejection is more than a political act. It is a protest of our souls against those who would have us forget the concepts of good and evil.

But what is amazing is that apart from all its writings, Communism has offered a multitude of examples for modern man to see. The tanks have rumbled through Budapest. This is nothing. The tanks roar into Czechoslovakia. This is nothing. No one else would have been forgiven, but Communism can be excused. With some kind of strange deliberation, as though God decided to punish them by taking away their reason, the Communists erected the Berlin Wall. It is indeed a monstrous symbol that demonstrates the true meaning of Communism. For fourteen years people have been machine-gunned there, and not only those who wanted to leave the happy Communist society. Recently some foreign boy from the Western side fell into the Spree River. Some people wanted to pull him out, but the East German border guards opened fire. 'No, no, don't save him.' And so this innocent boy drowned.

Has the Berlin Wall convinced anyone? No again. It is ignored. It's there, but it doesn't affect us: we'll never have a wall like that, and the tanks from Budapest and Prague won't come here either. On all the borders of the Communist countries, the European ones at least, you can find electronic devices for killing anyone who goes across. But people say, 'That doesn't threaten us either, we are not afraid of that.' In the Communist countries they have developed a system of forced treatment in insane asylums. That's nothing. We're living quietly. Three times a day – right at this very moment – the doctors are making their rounds and injecting substances that destroy the brain. Pay no attention to it. We'll continue to live in peace and quiet here.

There's a certain woman here named Angela Davis. I don't know if you are familiar with her in this country, but in our country, literally, for an entire year, we heard of nothing at all except Angela Davis. There was only Angela Davis in the whole world and she was suffering. We had our ears stuffed with Angela Davis. Little children in school were told to sign petitions in defence of Angela Davis. Little boys and girls, eight and nine years old, were asked to do this. She was set free, as you know. Although she didn't have too difficult a time in this country's jails, she came to recuperate in Soviet resorts. Some Soviet dissidents – but more important, a group of Czech dissidents – addressed an appeal to her: 'Comrade Davis, you were in prison. You know how unpleasant it is to sit in prison, especially when you consider yourself innocent. You have such great authority now. Could you help our Czech prisoners? Could you stand up for those people in Czechoslovakia who are being persecuted by the state?' Angela Davis answered, 'They deserve what they get. Let them remain in prison.' That is the face of Communism. That is the heart of Communism for you.

I would particularly like to remind you today that Communism develops in a straight line and as a single entity, without altering, as people now like to say. Lenin did indeed develop Marxism, but primarily along the lines of ideological intolerance. If you read Lenin, you will be astonished at how much hatred there was in him for the least deviation, whenever some view differed from his even by a hair's breadth. Lenin also developed Marxism in the direction of inhumanity. Before the October Revolution in Russia, Lenin wrote a book called *The Lessons of the Paris Commune*. There he analysed why the Paris Commune was defeated in 1871. His principal conclusion was that the Commune had not shot, had not killed enough of its enemies. It had destroyed too few people, at a time when it was necessary to kill entire classes and groups. And when he came to power, Lenin did just this.

And then the word 'Stalinism' was thought up. This is a term that became very popular. Even in the West they often say now, 'If only the Soviet

Union doesn't return to Stalinism.' But there was never any such thing as Stalinism. It was contrived by Khrushchev and his group in order to blame all the characteristic traits and principal defects of Communism on Stalin – it was a very effective move. But in reality Lenin had managed to give shape to all the main features before Stalin came to power. It is Lenin who deceived the peasants about their land, and the workers about self-management. He is the one who turned the trade unions into organs of oppression. He is the one who created the Cheka, the secret police, and the concentration camps. It is he who sent troops out to the border areas to crush any national movements for liberation and to set up an empire.

The only new thing that Stalin did was based on distrust. When it would have been enough – in order to instil general fear – to jail two people, he arrested a hundred. And those who succeeded Stalin merely turned to the previous tactic: if it is necessary to send two off to jail, then send two, not a hundred. In the eyes of the Party, Stalin's entire guilt lay elsewhere: he did not trust his own Communist Party. Due to this alone, the concept of Stalinism was devised. But Stalin had never deviated from the same basic line. They used to sculpt a bas-relief of Marx, Engels, Lenin, and Stalin all together; to this one could add Mao Tse-tung, Kim Il Sung, Ho Chi Minh; they are all in the same line of development.

The following theory is also accepted in the West. It is said that China is a sort of purified, puritanical type of Communism, one which has not degenerated. But China is simply a delayed phase of that so-called War Communism established by Lenin in Russia but which remained in force only until 1921. Lenin established it not at all because the military situation required it but because this is how he envisioned the future of their society. But when economic pressure required him to retreat, he introduced the so-called New Economic Policy and he retreated. In China this initial phase has simply lasted longer. China is characterised by all the same traits: massive compulsory labour which is not paid in accordance with its value; work on holidays; forced living in communes; and the incessant dinning of slogans and dogmas that abolish the human essence and deny all individuality to man.

The most frightening aspect of the world Communist system is its unity, its cohesion. Enrico Berlinguer said quite recently that the sun had set on the Comintern. Not at all. It hasn't set. Its energy has been transformed into electricity, which is now pulsing through underground cables. The sun of the Comintern today spreads its energy everywhere in the form of high-voltage electricity. Quite recently there was an incident when Western Communists indignantly denied that Portugal was operating on instructions from Moscow. Of course, Moscow also denied this. And then it was discovered that those very orders had been openly published in the Soviet magazine *Problems of Peace and Socialism*. These were the very instructions that Ponomarev had given. All the apparent differences among the Communist parties of the world are imaginary. All are united on one point: your social order must be destroyed.

Why should we be surprised if the world does

not understand this? Even the socialists, who are the closest to Communism, do not understand it. They cannot grasp the true nature of Communism. Recently, the leader of the Swedish socialists, Olof Palme, said that the only way that Communism can survive is by adopting the principles of democracy. That is the same thing as saying that the only way in which a wolf can survive is to stop eating meat and become a lamb. And yet Palme lives right next door, Sweden is quite close to the Soviet Union. I think that he, and Mitterrand, and the Italian socialists will live to see the day when they will be in the position that Portugal's Mario Soares is in today. Soares's situation, by the way, is not yet at its worst. An even more terrible future awaits him and his party. Only the Russian socialists – the Mensheviks and the Socialist Revolutionaries – could have told them of the fate that awaits them. But they cannot tell of it: they are all dead; they've all been killed. Read *The Gulag Archipelago*.

Of course, in the present situation the Communists have to use various disguises. Sometimes we hear words like the 'popular front', at other times 'dialogue with Christianity'. For Communists a dialogue with Christianity! In the Soviet Union this dialogue was a simple matter: they used machine guns and revolvers. And today, in Portugal, unarmed Catholics are stoned by the Communists. This is dialogue . . . And when the French and the Italian Communists say that they are going to have a dialogue, let them only get into power and we shall see what this dialogue will look like.

When I travelled to Italy this past April, I was

amazed to see hammers and sickles painted on the doors of churches, insults to priests scrawled on the doors of their houses. In general, offensive Communist graffiti cover the walls of Italian cities. This is today, before they have attained power. This is today . . . When Italy's leaders were in Moscow, Palmiro Togliatti agreed to all of Stalin's executions. Just let them have power in Italy and we shall see what the dialogue will look like then.

All of the Communist parties, upon attaining power, have become completely merciless. But at the stage before they achieve power, it is necessary to use disguises.

We Russians, with our historical experience, find it tragic to see what is going on in Portugal. We were always told, 'Well, this happened to you Russians. It's just that you couldn't maintain democracy in your country. You had it for eight months and then it was stifled. That's Eastern Europe for you.' But look at Portugal, at the very westernmost edge of Europe, and what do we see there? A kind of caricature, a slightly altered version of what happened in Russia. For us it sounds like a re-run. We recognise what's going on and can make the proper substitutions, placing our socialists in Soares's position.

The same things were said in Russia. The Bolsheviks pursued power under the slogan 'All Power to the Constituent Assembly'. But when the elections took place, they got 25 per cent of the vote, and so they dispersed the Constituent Assembly. The Communists in Portugal got 12 per cent of the vote. So they made their parliament entirely powerless. What irony: the socialists have won the elections. Soares is the leader of the victorious party. Yet he has been deprived of his own newspaper. Just imagine: the leader of a victorious party has been stripped of his own newspaper! And the fact that an assembly has been elected and will sit in session has no significance whatever. Yet the Western press writes seriously that the first free elections took place in Portugal. Lord save us from such free elections!

Specific instances of duplicity, of trickery, can change, of course, from one set of circumstances to another. But we recognise the Communist character in the episode when the Portuguese military leaders, who are allegedly not Communists, decided to settle the dispute within the newspaper *República* in the following manner. 'Come at twelve o'clock tomorrow,' they said, 'we'll open the doors for you and you settle it all as you see fit.' But they opened the doors at ten o'clock and for some reason only the Communists, not the socalists, knew of this. The Communists entered, burned all the incriminating documents, and then the socialists arrived. Ah yes, it was of course only an error. An accident, they didn't check the time . . .

These are the sort of tricks – and there are thousands – which make up the history of the Russian Revolution. There will be many more such incidents in Portugal. Take the following example: the current military leadership of Portugal, in order not to lose Western assistance (they have already ruined Portugal and there is nothing to eat, so they need help), have declared, 'Yes, we will keep our multi-party system.' And the unfortunate Soares, the leader of the victorious party, now has to demonstrate that he is pleased with this declaration in favour of a multi-party system. But on the same day the same source declared the construction of a classless society will begin immediately. Anyone who is the least bit familiar with Marxism knows that 'classless society' implies that there will not be any parties. That is to say, on the very same day they said: 'There will be a multi-party system and we will suppress every party.' But the former is heard and the latter is not. Everybody repeats only that there will be a multi-party system. This is a typical Communist method.

Portugal has, in effect, fallen out of NATO already. I don't wish to be a prophet of doom but these events are irreversible. Very shortly Portugal will be considered a member of the Warsaw Pact. It is painful to look at this tragic and ironic repetition of Communist methods at opposite ends of Europe, sixty years apart. In just a few months we see the stifling of a democracy which had only begun to get on its feet.

The question of war is also well elucidated in Communist and Marxist literature. Let me show you how Communism regards the question of war. I quote Lenin: 'We cannot support the slogan "Peace" since it is a totally muddled one and a hindrance to the revolutionary struggle.' (Letter to Alexandra Kollontai, July 1915.) 'To reject war in principle is un-Marxist. Who objectively stands to gain from the slogan "Peace"? In any case, not the revolutionary proletariat.' (Letter to Alexander Shliapnikov, November 1914.) 'There is no point in proposing a benign programme of pious wishes for peace without at the same time placing at the forefront the call for

(54)

illegal organisation and the summons to civil war.' This is Communism's view of war. War is necessary. War is an instrument for achieving a goal.

But unfortunately for Communism, this policy ran up against the American atomic bomb in 1945. Then the Communists changed their tactics and suddenly became advocates of peace at any cost. They started to convoke peace congresses, to circulate petitions for peace; and the Western world fell for this deceit. But the goal, the ideology, remained the same: to destroy your system, to destroy the way of life known in the West.

But they could not risk this in the face of your nuclear superiority. So they substituted one concept for another: what is not war, they said, is peace. That is, they opposed war to peace. But this is a mistake, only a part of the antithesis is opposed to the thesis. When an open war is impossible, oppression can continue quietly behind the scenes. Terrorism. Guerrilla warfare, violence, prisons, concentration camps. I ask you: is this peace?

The true antipode of peace is violence. And those who want peace in the world should remove not only war from the world but also violence. If there is no open war but there is still violence, that is not peace.

As long as in the Soviet Union, in China, and in other Communist countries there is no limit to the use of violence – and now we find India joining in (it appears that Indira Gandhi has learned much from her trip to Moscow; she has mastered these methods very well and is now adding another 400 million people to this continent of tyranny) –

as long as there is no limit to this use of violence, as long as nothing restrains it over this tremendous land mass (more than half of humanity), how can you consider yourselves secure?

America and Europe together are not yet an island in the ocean – I won't go so far as to say that. But America together with Europe is now a minority, and the process is still continuing. Until the public in those Communist countries can keep a check on the government and can have an opinion on what the government does – now it doesn't have the slightest idea what the government is up to – until that time comes, the West, and the world in general, has no guarantee at all.

We have another proverb in Russia: 'Catch on you will when you're tumbling downhill.'

I understand that you love freedom, but in our crowded world you have to pay a tax for freedom. You cannot love freedom for yourselves alone and quietly agree to a situation where the majority of humanity, spread over the greater part of the globe, is subjected to violence and oppression.

The Communist ideology is to destroy your social order. This has been their aim for 125 years and it has never changed; only the methods have changed a little. When there is détente, peaceful co-existence, and trade, they will still insist: the ideological war must continue! And what is ideological war? It is a concentration of hatred, a continued repetition of the oath to destroy the Western world. Just as in the Roman senate a famous speaker ended every speech with the statement: 'Furthermore, Carthage must be destroyed,' so today, with every act – détente, trade, or whatever – the Communist press, as well as thousands of speakers at closed lectures, all repeat: 'Furthermore, capitalism must be destroyed.'

It is easy to understand, it's only human that people living in prosperity doubt the necessity of taking steps – here and now in our state of prosperity – to defend themselves. For even in prosperity one must be on guard.

If I were to enumerate all the treaties that have been violated by the Soviet Union, it would take me another whole speech. I understand that when your statesmen sign some treaty with the Soviet Union or China you want to believe that it will be carried out. But the Poles who signed a treaty with the Communists in Riga in 1921 also wanted to believe that the treaty would be carried out, and they were stabbed in the back. Estonia, Latvia, and Lithuania, which signed treaties of friendship with the Soviet Union, also wanted to believe that they would be carried out, but these countries were all swallowed.

And the people who sign these treaties with you now – these very men and no others – simultaneously give orders for persons to be confined in mental hospitals and prisons. Why should they be different towards you? Surely not out of love for you? Why should they act honourably and nobly towards you when they crush their own people? The advocates of détente have yet to explain this.

You want to believe and so you cut down on your armies and your research. There used to be an Institute for the Study of the Soviet Union – at least there was one such institute. You know so little about the Soviet Union. It seems dark over there. These searchlights don't penetrate that far.

Knowing nothing, you eliminated the last genuine institute which could actually study this Soviet society, because there wasn't enough money to support it. But the Soviet Union is studying you. You are all wide open here, through the press and Congress. And they study you all the more, increasing the size of their staffs in the United States. They follow what's going on in your institutions. They attend meetings and conferences; they even visit congressional committees. They study everything.

Of course, peace treaties are very attractive to those who sign them. They strengthen one's prestige with the electorate. But the time will come when the names of these public figures will be erased from history. Nobody will remember them any longer. But the Western peoples will have to pay heavily for these overtrusting agreements.

Is it only a question of showing that détente is needed today, here and now? By no means. There are theoreticians who look very far into the future. The director of the Russian Institute of Columbia University, Marshall Shulman, at a meeting of the Senate Foreign Relations Committee, depicted a radiant future, stating that détente would ultimately lead to co-operation between the United States and the USSR in the establishment of a world order. But what sort of new order, in co-operation with insatiable totalitarianism, does this professor want to see established? It won't be your kind in any case.

The principal argument of the advocates of détente is well known: all of this must be done to avoid a nuclear war. But after all that has happened in recent years, I think I can set their minds at ease, and your minds at ease as well: there will not be any nuclear war. What for? Why should there be a nuclear war if for the last thirty years they have been breaking off as much of the West as they wanted – piece after piece, country after country, and the process keeps going on. In 1975 alone four countries were broken off. Four – three in Indochina plus India – and the process keeps going on, very rapidly too. One should be aware of how rapid the tempo is. But let us assume that finally the Western world will understand and say, 'No, not one step further.' What will happen then?

Let me direct your attention to the following fact: you have theoreticians who say, 'The US must stop the process of nuclear armament. We have enough already. Today America has enough nuclear weapons to destroy the other half of the world. Why should we need more than that?' Let the American nuclear specialists reason this way if they want, but for some reason the nuclear specialists of the Soviet Union – and the leaders of the Soviet Union – think differently. Ask your specialists! Leave aside their superiority in tanks and aeroplanes – where they surpass you by a factor of four, five, or seven. Take the SALT talks alone: in these negotiations your opponent is continually deceiving you. Either he is testing radar in a way which is forbidden by the agreement, or he is violating the limitations on the dimensions of missiles, or he is violating the limitations on their destructive force, or else he is violating the conditions on multiple warheads.

As the proverb says, 'Look before you leap, or you will have bruises to keep.'

At one time there was no comparison between the strength of the USSR and your own. Then it became equal to yours. Now, as all recognise, it is becoming superior to yours. Perhaps today the ratio is just greater than equal, but soon it will be 2 to 1. Then 3 to 1. Finally it will be 5 to 1. I'm not a specialist in this area, and I suppose you're not specialists either, but this can hardly be accidental. I think that if the armaments they had before were enough, they would not have driven things further. There must be some reason for it. With such nuclear superiority it will be possible to block the use of your weapons, and on some unlucky morning they will declare: 'Attention. We're sending our troops into Europe, and if you make a move, we will annihilate you.' And this ratio of 3 to 1 or 5 to 1 will have its effect: you will not make a move. Indeed, theoreticians will be found to say, 'If only we could have that blessed silence . . .'

To make a comparison with chess, this is like two players who are sitting at a chessboard, one of whom has a tremendously high opinion of himself and a rather low opinion of his opponent. Of course, he thinks he will outplay his opponent. He thinks he is so clever, so calculating, so inventive, that he will certainly win. He sits there, calculating his moves. With these two knights he will make four forks. He can hardly wait for his opponent to move. He's squirming on his chair from happiness. He takes off his glasses, wipes them, and puts them back on again. He doesn't even admit the possibility that his opponent may be more clever. He doesn't even see that his pawns are being taken one after the other and that his castle is under threat. It all seems to him, 'Aha, that's what we'll do. We'll set Moscow, Peking, Pyongyang, Hanoi one against the other.'

But what a joke! No one will do any such thing! In the meantime, you've been outplayed in West Berlin, you've been very skilfully outplayed in Portugal. In the Near East you're being outplayed. One shouldn't have such a low opinion of one's opponent.

But even if this chess player is able to win the game on the board, he forgets to raise his eyes, carried away as he is by the game; he forgets to look at his opponent and doesn't see that he has the eyes of a killer. And if this opponent cannot win the game on the board, he will take a club from behind his back and shatter the skull of our chess player, ending the game that way. Our very calculating chess player also forgets to raise his eyes to the barometer. It has fallen. He doesn't see that it's already dark outside, that clouds are gathering, that a hurricane is rising. That's what it means to be too self-confident in chess.

In addition to the grave political situation in the world today, we are also witnessing the emergence of a crisis of unknown nature, one completely new, and entirely non-political. We are approaching a major turning point in world history, in the history of civilisation. It has already been noted by specialists in various areas. I could compare it only with the turning from the Middle Ages to the modern era, a shift in our civilisation. It is a juncture at which settled concepts suddenly become hazy, lose their precise contours, at which our familiar and commonly used words lose their meaning, become empty shells, and methods which have been reliable for many centuries no longer work. It's the sort of turning point where the hierarchy of values which we have venerated, and which we use to determine what is important to us and what causes our hearts to beat is starting to rock and may collapse.

These two crises, the political crisis of today's world and the oncoming spiritual crisis, are occurring at the same time. It is our generation that will have to confront them. The leadership of your country, which is entering the third century of existence as a nation, will perhaps have to bear a burden greater than ever before in American history. Your leaders will need profound intuition, spiritual foresight, high qualities of mind and soul. May God grant that in those times you will have at the helm personalities as great as those who created your country.

In recent weeks, I have travelled through various states, and I am aware that the two cities in which I have made my addresses – Washington and New York – do not reflect your country as a whole with its tremendous diversity and possibilities. Just as old St Petersburg did not express the whole of Russia, just as Moscow does not reflect the Soviet Union of today, and just as Paris more than once abused its claim to represent all of France.

I was profoundly impressed by my contact with those places which are, and have always been, the wellsprings of your history. It makes one think that the men who created your country never lost sight of their moral bearings. They did not laugh at the absolute nature of the concepts of 'good' and 'evil'. Their practical policies were checked against that moral compass. And how surprising it is that a practical policy computed on the basis of moral considerations turned out to be the most farsighted and the most salutary. This is true even though in the short term one may wonder: why all this morality? Let's just get on with the immediate job.

The leaders who created your country never said: 'Let slavery reign right next door, and we will enter into détente with it as long as it doesn't come here.'

I have travelled enough through the different states of your country and in its various regions to have become convinced that the American heartland is healthy, strong, and broad in its outlook. I am convinced that these healthy, generous, and inexhaustible forces will help you to elevate the whole style of your government leadership.

Yet, when one travels in your country and sees your free and independent life, all the dangers which I have talked about today seem imaginary. I've talked to people, and I see this is so. In your wide-open spaces even I get a little infected, the dangers seem somehow unreal. On this continent it is hard to believe all the things which are happening in the world. But, ladies and gentlemen, this carefree life cannot continue in your country any more than in ours. The destinies of our two countries are going to be extremely difficult, and it is better to prepare for this beforehand.

I understand, I sense that you're tired. But you have not yet really suffered the terrible trials of the twentieth century which have rained down on the old continent. You're tired, but not as tired as we are, crushed for sixty years. You're tired, but the Communists who want to destroy your system are not; they're not tired at all.

I understand that this is the most unfavourable time to come to this country and to make this sort of address. But if it were a better, more appropriate time, there would be no need for me to speak.

Precisely because this is the worst possible time I have come to tell you about our experience over there. If our experience in the East could flow over to you by itself, it would be unnecessary for me to assume the unpleasant and inappropriate role of orator. I am a writer, and I would prefer to sit and write books.

But a concentration of world evil is taking place, full of hatred for humanity. It is fully determined to destroy your society. Must you wait until it comes to smash through your borders, until the young men of America have to fall defending the borders of their continent?

After my first address, as always, there were some superficial comments in the newspapers which did not really get to its essence. One of them asserted that I had come here with an appeal to the United States to liberate *us* from Communism. Anyone who has followed what I have said and written these many years, first in the Soviet Union and now in the West, will know that I've always said the exact opposite. I have appealed to my own countrymen – those whose courage has failed at difficult moments, and who have looked imploringly to the West – and urged them: 'Don't wait for assistance, and don't ask for it; we must stand on our own feet. The West has enough troubles without us. If they support us, they have our heartfelt thanks. But to plead for help, to appeal for it – never.'

I said the last time that two processes are occurring in the world today. One is a process of spiritual liberation in the USSR and in the other Communist countries. The second is the assistance being extended by the West to the Communist rulers, a process of concessions, of détente, of yielding whole countries. And I only said: 'Remember, we have to pull ourselves up by our own efforts – but if you do defend us, you defend your own future.'

We are slaves there from birth. We are born slaves. I'm not young any more, and I myself was born a slave; this is even more true for those who are younger. We are slaves, but we are striving for freedom. You, however, were born free. So why do you let yourselves be used by slavery? Why do you help our slaveowners?

In my last address I only requested one thing and I make the same request now: when they bury us in the ground alive – I compared the forthcoming European agreement with a mass grave for all the countries of Eastern Europe – as you know, this is a very unpleasant sensation: your mouth gets filled with earth while you're still alive – please do not send them shovels. Please do not send them the latest earth-moving equipment.

By a peculiar coincidence, the very day when I was giving my address in Washington, Mikhail Suslov was talking with your senators in the

Kremlin. And he said, 'In fact, the significance of our trade is more political than economic. We can get along without your trade.' That's a lie. The whole existence of our slaveowners from beginning to end relies on Western economic assistance. As I said the last time, beginning with the first spare parts used to reconstruct our factories in the 1920s, from the construction in Magnitostroy, Dneprostroy, the automobile and tractor factories built during the first Five-Year Plans, on into the postwar years and to this day, what they need from you is economically absolutely indispensable – not politically, but economically indispensable – to the Soviet system. The Soviet economy has an extremely low level of efficiency. What is done here by a few people, by a few machines, in our country takes tremendous crowds of workers and enormous amounts of material. Therefore, the Soviet economy cannot deal with every problem at once: war, space (which is part of the war effort), heavy industry, light industry, and at the same time the need to feed and clothe its own population. The forces of the entire Soviet economy are concentrated on war, where you don't help them. But everything lacking, everything needed to fill the gaps, everything necessary to feed the people, or for other types of industry, they get from you. So indirectly you are helping their military preparations. You are helping the Soviet police state.

I'll give you an example of the clumsiness of the Soviet economy. What kind of country is it, what kind of great power, with tremendous military potential, that conquers outer space but has nothing to sell? All heavy equipment, all complex and delicate technology, is purchased abroad. Then it must be an agricultural country? Not at all; it also has to buy grain. What then can we sell? What kind of economy is it? Can we sell anything which has been created by socialism? No! Only that which God put in the Russian ground at the very beginning, that's what we squander and that's what we sell. When all this comes to an end, there won't be anything left to sell.

The president of the AFL-CIO, George Meany, has quite rightly said that it is not loans which the United States gives to the Soviet Union, it is economic assistance, foreign aid, given at a lower interest level than American workers can get for their home mortgages. That is direct aid.

But this is not all. I said in my last address, and would like to repeat, that we have to look at every event from the other point of view – from the point of view of the Soviet Union. Our country takes your assistance, but in the schools they teach and in the newspapers they write and in lectures they say: 'Look at the Western world, it's beginning to rot. Look at the economy of the Western world, it's coming to an end. The great predictions of Marx, Engels, and Lenin are coming true. Capitalism is breathing its last. It's already dead. And our socialist economy is flourishing. It has demonstrated once and for all the triumph of Communism.' I think, ladies and gentlemen, and I particularly address those of you who have a socialist outlook, that we should at least permit this socialist economy to prove its superiority. Let's allow it to show that it is advanced, that it is omnipotent, that it has defeated

you, that it has overtaken you. Let us not interfere with it. Let us stop selling to it and giving it
loans. If it's all that powerful, then let it stand on
its own feet for ten or fifteen years. Then we will
see what it looks like. I can tell you what it will
look like. I am being quite serious now. When
the Soviet economy will no longer be able to deal
with everything, it will have to reduce its military
preparations. It will have to abandon the useless
space effort and it will have to feed and clothe its
own people. And the system will be forced to
relax.

Thus, all I ask you is that as long as this Soviet
economy is so proud, so flourishing, and yours is
so rotten and so moribund – stop helping it.
When has a cripple ever helped along an athlete?

Another distortion appeared in your press with
respect to my last address. Someone wrote that
'One more advocate of the Cold War has come
here. One more person has arrived to call on us
to resume the Cold War.' That is a misunder-
standing. The Cold War – the war of hatred – is
still going on, but only on the Communist side.
What is the Cold War? It's a war of abuse and
they still abuse you. They trade with you, they
sign agreements and treaties, but they still abuse
you, they still curse you. In sources which you
can read, and even more in those which are un-
available to you, and which you don't hear of, in
the depths of the Soviet Union, the Cold War has
never stopped, not for one second. They never
call you anything but 'American imperialists'.
One day, if they want, all the Soviet newspapers
could say that America wants to subjugate the
world and our people would have nowhere to get

any other information. Do I call upon you to return to the Cold War? By no means, God forbid! What for? The only thing I'm asking you to do is to give the Soviet economy a chance to develop. Do not bury us in the ground, just let the Soviet economy develop, and then let's see.

But can the free and varied Western system follow such a policy? Can all the Western countries together say: It's true, let us stop competing. Let us stop playing up to them. Let us stop elbowing each other and clamouring, 'Me, me, let me have a concession, please give it to me . . .' It's very possible that this cannot be done. And if this sort of unity cannot be achieved in the West, if, in the frenzied competition of one company with another, they will continue to rush in loans and advanced technology, if they will present earth-moving equipment to our gravediggers, then I'm afraid that Lenin will turn out to have been right. He said: 'The bourgeoisie will sell us rope, and then we will let the bourgeoisie hang itself.'

In ancient times trade used to begin with the meeting of two persons who had come out of a forest or had arrived by sea. They would show one another that they didn't have a stone or club in their hand, that they were unarmed; as a sign of this, each extended an open hand. This was the beginning of the handclasp. Today's word 'détente' literally means a reduction in the tension of a taut rope. (What an ominous coincidence: a rope again!)

So 'détente' means a relaxation of tension. But I would say that what we need instead is an image of the open hand. Relations between the Soviet Union and the United States should be such that there would be no deceit in the question of armaments, that there would be no concentration camps, no psychiatric wards for healthy people. Relations should be such that the throats of our women would no longer be constricted with tears, that there would be an end to the incessant ideological warfare waged against you, and that an address such as mine today would in no way be an exception.

People would simply be able to come to you from the Soviet Union, from China, and from other Communist countries and would be able to talk freely, without any tutoring from the KGB, without any special approval from the Central Committee of the Party. Rather, they would simply come of their own accord and would tell you the truth about what is going on in these countries.

This would be, I say, a period in which we would be able to present 'open hands' to each other.

15 July 1975

This speech was delivered by Mr
Solzhenitsyn to members of the Senate
and the House of Representatives in
Washington, DC.

GENTLEMEN:
Here, in the Senate Office Building I must begin
by saying that I have not forgotten the high, indeed the exceptional, honour paid me by the
United States Senate in twice endeavouring to
declare me an honorary citizen of the United
States.

I take this to mean that you had in mind not
only myself as an individual but also the millions
of my fellow countrymen who have been deprived
of rights, and even those in the other Communist
countries, those millions who have never been
able, and are still unable, to express their opinions
in the press, in parliaments, or at international
conferences.

As I convey to you my gratitude for the
decisions of the United States Senate concerning
myself, I am all the more conscious of my responsibility as a spokesman for those others, a responsibility almost too massive for the shoulders of a
single human being. But I have never lost sight
of the suffering, the striving and the hopes of

those voiceless millions, and have had no aim in life other than to give them expression, and this lends me strength for my public appearances in this country and for my appearance before you today. For the time being, there are few people in the Communist countries who speak out publicly, but millions understand the loathsome nature of the system and feel a revulsion towards it. Whoever can 'votes with his feet', simply fleeing from this mass violence and destruction.

I see before me today not only members of the Senate but also a group of Representatives. Thus, I am speaking for the first time to participants in your country's legislative process whose influence in recent years has spread far beyond the limits of American history.

In virtually every respect, our Russian historical experience has been almost the opposite of yours. The innumerable events that have befallen us in the twentieth century have enriched our Russian experience in an unfortunate way, and now they seem to confront you from the future. It is that much more crucial that we persistently and sincerely try to convey our respective experience to one another. One of today's most terrible dangers is precisely that the destinies of the world are entangled as never before, so that events or mistakes in one part of the world are immediately felt in all the others. At the same time, the exchange of information and of opinions between populations is blocked by iron barriers on the one side, while on the other it is distorted by distance, paucity of information, narrowness of outlook, or deliberate misrepresentation by observers and commentators.

In my few addresses in your country I have attempted to break through that wall of disastrous unawareness or nonchalant superiority. I have tried to convey to your countrymen the constrained breathing of the inhabitants of Eastern Europe in these weeks when an amicable agreement of diplomatic shovels will inter in a common grave bodies that are still breathing. I have tried to explain to Americans that 1973, the tender dawn of détente, was precisely the year when the starvation rations in Soviet prisons and concentration camps were reduced even further. And in recent months, when more and more Western speechmakers have pointed to the beneficial consequences of détente, the Soviet Union has adopted a novel and important improvement in its system of punishment: to retain their glorious supremacy in the invention of forced-labour camps, Soviet prison specialists have now established a new form of solitary confinement – forced labour in solitary cells. That means cold, hunger, lack of fresh air, insufficient light, and impossible work norms; the failure to fulfil these norms is punished by confinement under even more brutal conditions.

Alas, such is human nature that we never feel the sufferings of others, and they never darken our temporary well-being, until they become our own. I am not certain that in my addresses here I have succeeded in conveying the breath of that terrible reality to a complacently prosperous American society. But I have done what I could and what I consider my duty. So much the worse if the justice of my warnings becomes evident only some years hence.

Your country has just recently passed through

the extended ordeal of Vietnam, which exhausted and divided your society. I can say with certainty that this ordeal was the least of a long chain of similar trials which awaits you in the near future.

Whether or not the United States so desires, it has risen to the peak of world history and carries the burden of leadership for at least half the world. The United States has not had a thousand-year preparation for this task. Perhaps the two hundred years of your existence has not been time enough to produce a sense of national awareness. Meanwhile, the load of obligations and responsibilities has fallen on you unbidden.

That is why, members of the Senate and of the House of Representatives, each one of you is not just an ordinary member of an ordinary parliament – you have been elevated to a particularly high position in the contemporary world. I would like to convey to you how we, the subjects of Communist states, look upon your words, deeds, proposals, and enactments, which are made known to the world through the media. We sometimes greet them with passionate approval, at other times with horror and despair. But we never have a chance to respond aloud.

Perhaps some of you, in your minds, still consider yourselves to represent only your state or party. But, from over there, from afar, we do not perceive these differences. We do not look upon you as Democrats or Republicans, or as representatives of the Eastern Seaboard or the West Coast or the Midwest; we see you as statesmen, each of whom will play a direct and decisive role in the further course of world history, as it proceeds towards tragedy or salvation.

In the oncoming conjunction of a world political crisis with the present changes in a humanity exhausted and choked by a false hierarchy of values, you or your successors on Capitol Hill will have to confront – you are already facing – problems of overwhelming difficulty, incomparably greater than the short-term calculations of diplomacy, of inter-party struggles, or of the clash between President and Congress. There is but one choice: to rise to the tasks of the age.

Very soon, only too soon, your country will stand in need of not just exceptional men but of *great* men. Find them in your souls. Find them in your hearts. Find them in the depths of your country.

8 June 1978

Mr Solzhenitsyn delivered this speech at
the annual commencement ceremony at
Harvard University.

I am sincerely happy to be here with you on the
occasion of the 327th commencement of this old
and illustrious university. My congratulations
and best wishes to all of today's graduates.

Harvard's motto is 'Veritas'. Many of you have
already found out and others will find out in the
course of their lives that truth eludes us as soon
as our concentration begins to flag, all the while
leaving the illusion that we are continuing to
pursue it. This is the source of much discord.
Also, the truth seldom is sweet; it is almost in-
variably bitter. A measure of bitter truth is
included in my speech today, but I offer it as a
friend, not as an adversary.

Three years ago in the United States I said certain things that were rejected and appeared un-
acceptable. Today, however, many people agree
with what I then said . . .

A World Split Apart

The split in today's world is perceptible even to
a hasty glance. Any of our contemporaries readily

identifies two world powers, each of them quiet
capable of utterly destroying the other. However, the understanding of the split too often is
limited to this political conception: the illusion
according to which danger may be abolished
through successful diplomatic negotiations or by
achieving a balance of armed forces. The truth is
that the split is both more profound and more
alienating, that the rifts are more numerous than
one can see at first glance. These deep manifold
splits bear the danger of equally manifold disaster
for all of us, in accordance with the ancient truth
that a kingdom – in this case, our Earth – divided
against itself cannot stand.

Contemporary Worlds

There is the concept of the Third World: thus,
we already have three worlds. Undoubtedly, however, the number is even greater; we are just too
far away to see. Every ancient and deeply rooted,
self-contained culture, especially if it is spread
over a wide part of the earth's surface, constitutes
a self-contained world, full of riddles and sur-
prises to Western thinking. As a minimum, we
must include in this category China, India, the
Muslim world and Africa, if indeed we accept the
approximation of viewing the latter two as uni-
form. For one thousand years Russia belonged
to such a category, although Western thinking
systematically committed the mistake of denying
its special character and therefore never understood it, just as today the West does not understand Russia in Communist captivity. And while
it may be that in past years Japan has increasingly
become, in effect, a Far West, drawing ever closer

to Western ways (I am no judge here), Israel, I think, should not be reckoned as part of the West, if only because of the decisive circumstance that its state system is fundamentally linked to religion.

How short a time ago, relatively, the small world of modern Europe was easily seizing colonies all over the globe, not only without anticipating any real resistance, but usually with contempt for any possible values in the conquered peoples' approach to life. On the face of it, it was an overwhelming success, with no geographic limits. Western society expanded in a triumph of human independence and power. And all of a sudden the twentieth century brought the clear realisation of this society's fragility. We now see that the conquests proved to be shortlived and precarious, and this, in turn, points to defects in the Western view of the world which led to these conquests. Relations with the former colonial world now have switched to the opposite extreme and the Western world often exhibits an excess of obsequiousness, but it is difficult yet to estimate the size of the bill which former colonial countries will present to the West and it is difficult to predict whether the surrender not only of its last colonies, but of everything it owns will be sufficient for the West to clear this account.

Convergence

But the persisting blindness of superiority continues to hold the belief that all the vast regions of our planet should develop and mature to the level of contemporary Western systems, the best in theory and the most attractive in practice; that all those other worlds are but temporarily prevented by wicked leaders or by severe crises or by their own barbarity and incomprehension from pursuing Western pluralistic democracy and adopting the Western way of life. Countries are judged on the merits of their progress in that direction. But in fact such a conception is a fruit of Western incomprehension of the essence of other worlds, a result of mistakenly measuring them all with a Western yardstick. The real picture of our planet's development bears little resemblance to all this.

The anguish of a divided world gave birth to the theory of convergence between the leading Western countries and the Soviet Union. It is a soothing theory which overlooks the fact that these worlds are not at all evolving towards each other and that neither one can be transformed into the other without violence. Besides, convergence inevitably means acceptance of the other side's defects, and this can hardly suit anyone.

If I were today addressing an audience in my country, in my examination of the overall pattern of the world's rifts I would have concentrated on the calamities of the East. But since my forced exile in the West has now lasted four years and since my audience is a Western one, I think it may be of greater interest to concentrate on certain aspects of the contemporary West, such as I see them.

A Decline in Courage

A decline in courage may be the most striking feature which an outside observer notices in the West today. The Western world has lost its civic courage, both as a whole and separately, in each country, in each government, in each political party and, of course, in the United Nations. Such a decline in courage is particularly noticeable among the ruling and intellectual elites, causing an impression of a loss of courage by the entire society. There remain many courageous individuals, but they have no determining influence on public life. Political and intellectual functionaries exhibit this depression, passivity and perplexity in their actions and in their statements, and even more so in their self-serving rationales as to how realistic, reasonable and intellectually and even morally justified it is to base state policies on weakness and cowardice. And the decline in courage, at times attaining what could be termed a lack of manhood, is ironically emphasised by occasional outbursts of boldness and inflexibility on the part of those same functionaries when dealing with weak governments and with countries that lack support, or with doomed currents which clearly cannot offer any resistance. But they get tongue-tied and paralysed when they deal with powerful governments and threatening forces, with aggressors and international terrorists.

Must one point out that from ancient times a decline in courage has been considered the beginning of the end?

Well-being

When the modern Western states were being formed, it was proclaimed as a principle that governments are meant to serve man and that man lives in order to be free and pursue happiness. (See, for example, the American Declaration of Independence.) Now at last during past decades technical and social progress has permitted the realisation of such aspirations: the welfare state. Every citizen has been granted the desired freedom and material goods in such quantity and of such quality as to guarantee in theory the achievement of happiness, in the debased sense of the word which has come into being during those same decades. (In the process, however, one psychological detail has been overlooked: the constant desire to have still more things and a still better life, and the struggle to this end imprints many Western faces with worry and even depression, though it is customary to carefully conceal such feelings. This active and tense competition comes to dominate all human thought and does not in the least open a way to free spiritual development.) The individual's independence from many types of state pressure has been guaranteed; the majority of the people have been granted well-being to an extent their fathers and grandfathers could not even dream about; it has become possible to raise young people according to these ideals, preparing them for and summoning them towards physical bloom, happiness, possession of material goods, money and leisure, towards an almost unlimited freedom in the choice of pleasures. So who should now renounce all this, why and for the sake of what should one risk one's precious life in defence of the common good, and particularly in the nebulous case when the security of one's nation must be defended in an as yet distant land?

Even biology tells us that a high degree of habitual well-being is not advantageous to a living organism. Today, well-being in the life of Western society has begun to reveal its pernicious mask.

Legalistic Life

Western society has chosen for itself the organisation best suited to its purposes and one I might call legalistic. The limits of human rights and rightness are determined by a system of laws; such limits are very broad. People in the West have acquired considerable skill in using, interpreting and manipulating law (though laws tend to be too complicated for an average person to understand without the help of an expert). Every conflict is solved according to the letter of the law and this is considered to be the ultimate solution. If one is right from a legal point of view, nothing more is required, nobody may mention that one could still not be entirely right, and urge self-restraint or a renunciation of these rights, call for sacrifice and selfless risk: this would simply sound absurd. Voluntary self-restraint is almost unheard of: everybody strives towards further expansion to the extreme limit of the legal frames. (An oil company is legally blameless when it buys up an invention of a new type of energy in order to prevent its use. A food product manufacturer is legally blameless when he poisons his product to make it last longer: after all, people are free not to purchase it.)

I have spent all my life under a Communist regime and I will tell you that a society without any objective legal scale is a terrible one indeed. But a society with no other scale but the legal one is also less than worthy of man. A society based on the letter of the law and never reaching any higher fails to take advantage of the full range of human possibilities. The letter of the law is too cold and formal to have a beneficial influence on society. Whenever the tissue of life is woven of legalistic relationships, this creates an atmosphere of spiritual mediocrity that paralyses man's noblest impulses.

And it will be simply impossible to bear up to the trials of this threatening century with nothing but the supports of a legalistic structure.

The Direction of Freedom

Today's Western society has revealed the inequality between the freedom for good deeds and the freedom for evil deeds. A statesman who wants to achieve something important and highly constructive for his country has to move cautiously and even timidly; thousands of hasty (and irresponsible) critics cling to him at all times; he is constantly rebuffed by parliament and the press. He has to prove that his every step is well-founded and absolutely flawless. Indeed, any outstanding, truly great person who has unusual and unexpected initiatives in mind does not get any chance to assert himself; dozens of traps will be set for him from the beginning. Thus mediocrity triumphs under the guise of democratic restraints.

It is feasible and easy everywhere to undermine administrative power and it has in fact been drastically weakened in all Western countries. The defence of individual rights has reached such extremes as to make society as a whole defenceless against certain individuals. It is time, in the

West, to defend not so much human rights as human obligations.

On the other hand, destructive and irresponsible freedom has been granted boundless space. Society has turned out to have scarce defence against the abyss of human decadence, for example against the misuse of liberty for moral violence against young people, such as motion pictures full of pornography, crime and horror. This is all considered to be part of freedom and to be counterbalanced, in theory, by the young people's right not to look and not to accept. Life organised legalistically has thus shown its inability to defend itself against the corrosion of Evil.

And what shall we say about the dark realms of overt criminality? Legal limits (especially in the United States) are broad enough to encourage not only individual freedom but also certain individual crimes. The culprit can go unpunished or obtain undeserved leniency – all with the support of thousands of defenders in the society. When a government earnestly undertakes to root out terrorism, public opinion immediately accuses it of violating the terrorists' civil rights. There is quite a number of such cases.

This tilt of freedom towards Evil has come about gradually, but it evidently stems from a humanistic and benevolent concept according to which man – the master of this world – does not bear any evil within himself, and all the defects of life are caused by misguided social systems which must therefore be corrected. Yet, strangely enough, though the best social conditions have been achieved in the West, there still remains a great deal of crime, there even is considerably more of it than in the destitute and lawless Soviet society. (There is a multitude of prisoners in our camps who are termed criminals, but most of them never committed any crime; they merely tried to defend themselves against a lawless state by resorting to means outside the legal framework.)

The Direction of the Press

The press, too, of course, enjoys the widest freedom. (I shall be using the word press to include all the media.) But what use does it make of it?

Here again, the overriding concern is not to infringe the letter of the law. There is no moral responsibility for distortion or disproportion. What sort of responsibility does a journalist or a newspaper have to the readership or to history? If they have misled public opinion by inaccurate information or wrong conclusions, even if they have contributed to mistakes on a state level, do we know of any case of open regret voiced by the same journalist or the same newspaper? No, this would damage sales. A nation may be the worse for such a mistake, but the journalist always gets away with it. It is most likely that he will start writing the exact opposite to his previous statements with renewed aplomb.

Because instant and credible information is required, it becomes necessary to resort to guess-work, rumours and suppositions to fill in the voids, and none of them will ever be refuted; they settle into the readers' memory. How many hasty, immature, superficial and misleading judgments are expressed every day, confusing readers, and are then left hanging? The press has the power to mould public opinion, and also to pervert it. Thus we may see terrorists treated as heroes, or secret matters pertaining to the nation's defence publicly revealed, or we may witness shameless intrusion into the privacy of well-known people according to the slogan that 'Everyone is entitled to know everything'. (But this is a false slogan of a false era: far greater in value is the forfeited right of people *not to know*, not to have their divine souls stuffed with gossip, nonsense, vain talk. A person who works and leads a meaningful life has no need for this excessive and burdening flow of information.)

Hastiness and superficiality – these are the psychic diseases of the twentieth century and more than anywhere else this is manifested in the press. In-depth analysis of a problem is anathema to the press, it is contrary to its nature. The press merely picks out sensational formulas.

Such as it is, however, the press has become the greatest power within the Western countries, exceeding that of the legislature, the executive and the judiciary. Yet one would like to ask: according to what law has it been elected and to whom is it responsible? In the Communist East, a journalist is frankly appointed as a state official. But who has voted Western journalists into their positions of power, for how long a time and with what prerogatives?

There is yet another surprise for someone coming from the totalitarian East with its rigorously unified press: one gradually discovers a common trend of preferences within the Western press as a whole (the spirit of the time), generally accepted patterns of judgment and maybe common corporate interests, the sum effect being not competition but unification. Unrestrained freedom exists for the press, but not for the readership because newspapers mostly transmit in a forceful and emphatic way those opinions which do not too openly contradict their own and that general trend.

A Fashion in Thinking

Without any censorship in the West, fashionable trends of thought and ideas are fastidiously separated from those which are not fashionable and the latter, without ever being forbidden, have little chance of finding their way into periodicals or books or being heard in colleges. Your scholars are free in the legal sense, but they are hemmed in by the idols of the prevailing fad. There is no open violence as in the East; however, a selection dictated by fashion and the need to accommodate mass standards frequently prevents the most independent-minded persons from contributing to public life and gives rise to dangerous herd instincts that block successful development. In America, I have received letters from highly intelligent persons, maybe a teacher in a far away small college, who could do much for the renewal and salvation of his country, but the country cannot hear him because the media will not provide him with a forum. This gives birth to strong mass prejudices, to a blindness which is perilous in our dynamic era. An example is the self-deluding interpretation of the state of affairs in the contemporary world that functions as a sort of a petrified armour around people's minds, to such a degree that human voices from seventeen countries of Eastern Europe and Eastern Asia cannot pierce it. It will be broken only by the inexorable crowbar of events.

I have mentioned a few traits of Western life which surprise and shock a new arrival to this world. The purpose and scope of this speech will not allow me to continue such a survey, in particular to look into the impact of these characteristics on important aspects of a nation's life such as elementary education, advanced education in the humanities and art.

Socialism

It is almost universally recognised that the West shows all the world the way to successful economic development, even though in past years it has been sharply offset by chaotic inflation. However, many people living in the West are dissatisfied with their own society. They despise it or accuse it of no longer being up to the level of maturity attained by mankind. And this causes many to sway towards socialism, which is a false and dangerous current.

I hope that no one present will suspect me of expressing my personal criticism of the Western system in order to suggest socialism as an alternative. No, with the experience of a country where socialism has been realised, I shall certainly not speak for such an alternative. The mathematician Igor Shafarevich, a member of the Soviet Academy of Science, has written a brilliantly argued book entitled *Socialism*; this is a penetrating historical analysis demonstrating that socialism of any type and shade leads to a total destruction of the human spirit and to a levelling of mankind into death. Shafarevich's book was published in France almost two years ago and so far no one has been found to refute it. It will shortly be published in English in the US.

Not a Model

But should I be asked, instead, whether I would propose the West, such as it is today, as a model to my country, I would frankly have to answer negatively. No, I could not recommend your society as an ideal for the transformation of ours. Through deep suffering, people in our country have now achieved a spiritual development of such intensity that the Western system in its present state of spiritual exhaustion does not look attractive. Even those characteristics of your life which I have just enumerated are extremely saddening.

A fact which cannot be disputed is the weakening of human personality in the West, while in the East it has become firmer and stronger. Six decades for our people and three decades for the people of Eastern Europe; during that time we have been through a spiritual training far in advance of Western experience. The complex and deadly crush of life has produced stronger, deeper and more interesting personalities than those generated by standardised Western well-being. Therefore, if our society were to be transformed into yours, it would mean an improvement in certain aspects, but also a change for the worse on some particularly significant points. Of course, a society cannot remain in an abyss of lawlessness as is the case in our country. But it is also demeaning for it to stay on such a soulless and smooth plane of legalism as is the case in yours. After the suffering of decades of violence and oppression, the human soul longs for things higher, warmer and purer than those offered by today's mass living habits, introduced as by a calling card by the revolting invasion of commercial advertising, by TV stupor and by intolerable music.

All this is visible to numerous observers from all the worlds of our planet. The Western way of life is less and less likely to become the leading model.

There are telltale symptoms by which history gives warning to a threatened or perishing society. Such are, for instance, a decline of the arts or a lack of great statesmen. Indeed, sometimes the warnings are quite explicit and concrete. The centre of your democracy and of your culture is left without electric power for a few hours only, and all of a sudden crowds of American citizens start looting and creating havoc. The smooth surface film must be very thin, then, the social system quite unstable and unhealthy.

But the fight for our planet, physical and spiritual, a fight of cosmic proportions, is not a vague matter of the future; it has already started. The forces of Evil have begun their decisive offensive; you can feel their pressure, yet your screens and publications are full of prescribed smiles and raised glasses. What is the joy about?

Shortsightedness

Very well-known representatives of your society, such as George Kennan, say: 'We cannot apply moral criteria to politics.' Thus we mix good and evil, right and wrong and make space for the absolute triumph of absolute Evil in the world. On the contrary, only moral criteria can help the West against Communism's well-planned world strategy. There are no other criteria. Practical or occasional considerations of any kind will inevitably be swept away by strategy. After a certain level of the problem has been reached, legalistic thinking induces paralysis; it prevents one from seeing the scale and the meaning of events.

In spite of the abundance of information, or maybe partly because of it, the West has great difficulty in finding its bearings amid contemporary events. There have been naïve predictions by some American experts who believed that Angola would become the Soviet Union's Vietnam or that the impudent Cuban expeditions in Africa would best be stopped by special US courtesy to Cuba. Kennan's advice to his own country – to begin unilateral disarmament – belongs to the same category. If you only knew how the youngest of the officials in Moscow's Old Square* roar with laughter at your political wizards! As to Fidel Castro, he openly scorns the United States, boldly sending his troops to distant adventures from his country right next to yours.

However, the most cruel mistake occurred with the failure to understand the Vietnam war. Some people sincerely wanted all wars to stop just as soon as possible; others believed that the way should be left open for national, or Com-

* The Old Square in Moscow (Staraya Ploshchad') is the place where the Headquarters of the Central Committee of the CPSU are located; it is the real name of what in the West is conventionally referred to as the Kremlin.

munist, self-determination in Vietnam (or in Cambodia, as we see today with particular clarity). But in fact members of the US anti-war movement became accomplices in the betrayal of Far Eastern nations, in the genocide and the suffering today imposed on thirty million people there. Do these convinced pacifists now hear the moans coming from there? Do they understand their responsibility today? Or do they prefer not to hear? The American intelligentsia lost its nerve and as a consequence the danger has come much closer to the United States. But there is no awareness of this. Your shortsighted politician who signed the hasty Vietnam capitulation seemingly gave America a carefree breathing pause; however, a hundredfold Vietnam now looms over you. That small Vietnam had been a warning and an occasion to mobilise the nation's courage. But if the full might of America suffered a fully-fledged defeat at the hands of a small Communist half-country, how can the West hope to stand firm in the future?

I have said on another occasion that in the twentieth century Western democracy has not won any major war by itself; each time it shielded itself with an ally possessing a powerful land army, whose philosophy it did not question. In World War II against Hitler, instead of winning the conflict with its own forces, which would certainly have been sufficient, Western democracy raised up another enemy, one that would prove worse and more powerful, since Hitler had neither the resources nor the people, nor the ideas with broad appeal, nor such a large number of supporters in the West – a fifth column – as the Soviet

Union possessed. Some Western voices already have spoken of the need of a protective screen against hostile forces in the next world conflict; in this case, the shield would be China. But I would not wish such an outcome to any country in the world. First of all it is again a doomed alliance with Evil; it would grant the United States a respite, but when at a later date China with its billion people would turn around armed with American weapons, America itself would fall victim to a Cambodia-style genocide.

Loss of Will

And yet – no weapons, no matter how powerful, can help the West until it overcomes its loss of willpower. In a state of psychological weakness, weapons even become a burden for the capitulating side. To defend oneself, one must also be ready to die; there is little such readiness in a society raised in the cult of material wellbeing. Nothing is left, in this case, but concessions, attempts to gain time and betrayal. Thus at the shameful Belgrade Conference free Western diplomats in their weakness surrendered the line of defence for which enslaved members of the Helsinki Watch Groups are sacrificing their lives.

Western thinking has become conservative: the world situation must stay as it is at any cost, there must be no changes. This debilitating dream of a *status quo* is the symptom of a society that has ceased to develop. But one must be blind in order not to see that the oceans no longer belong to the West, while the land under its domination keeps shrinking. The two so-called world wars (they were by far not on a world scale, not yet) constituted the internal self-destruction of the small progressive West, which has thus prepared its own end. The next war (which does not have to be an atomic one, I do not believe it will be) may well bury Western civilisation for ever.

In the face of such a danger, with such historical values in your past, with such a high level of attained freedom and, apparently, of devotion to it, how is it possible to lose to such an extent the will to defend oneself?

Humanism and its Consequences

How has this unfavourable relation of forces come about? How did the West decline from its triumphal march to its present debility? Have there been fatal turns and losses of direction in its development? It does not seem so. The West kept advancing steadily in accordance with its proclaimed social intentions, hand in hand with a dazzling progress in technology. And all of a sudden it found itself in its present state of weakness.

This means that the mistake must be at the root, at the very foundation of thought in modern times. I refer to the prevailing Western view of the world which was born in the Renaissance and has found political expression since the Age of Enlightenment. It became the basis for political and social doctrine and could be called rationalistic humanism or humanistic autonomy: the proclaimed and practised autonomy of man from any higher force above him. It could also be called anthropocentricity, with man seen as the centre of all.

The turn introduced by the Renaissance was

probably inevitable historically: the Middle Ages had come to a natural end by exhaustion, having become an intolerable despotic repression of man's physical nature in favour of the spiritual one. But then, we recoiled from the Spirit and embraced all that is material, excessively and incommensurately. The humanistic way of thinking, which had proclaimed itself our guide, did not admit the existence of intrinsic evil in man nor did it see any task higher than the attainment of happiness on earth. It started modern Western civilisation on the dangerous trend of worshipping man and his material needs. Everything beyond physical well-being and the accumulation of material goods, all other human requirements and characteristics of a subtler and higher nature, were left outside the area of attention of state and social systems, as if human life did not have any higher meaning. Thus, gaps were left open for Evil and its draughts blow freely today. Mere freedom *per se* does not in the least solve all the problems of human life and even adds a number of new ones.

And yet, in early democracies, as in American democracy at the time of its birth, all individual human rights were granted on the ground that man is God's creature. That is, freedom was given to the individual conditionally, on the assumption of his constant religious responsibility. Such was the heritage of the preceding one thousand years. Two hundred or even fifty years ago, it would have seemed quite impossible, in America, that an individual be granted boundless freedom with no purpose, simply for the satisfaction of his whims. Subsequently, however, all such limitations were eroded everywhere in the West; a total emancipation occurred from the moral heritage of Christian centuries with their great reserves of mercy and sacrifice. State systems were becoming ever more materialistic. The West has finally achieved the rights of man, and even to excess, but man's sense of responsibility to God and society has grown dimmer and dimmer. In the past decades, the legalistic selfishness of the Western approach to the world has reached its peak and the world found itself in a harsh spiritual crisis and a political impasse. All the celebrated technological achievements of Progress, including the conquest of outer space, do not redeem the twentieth century's moral poverty, which no one could have imagined even as late as the nineteenth century.

An Unexpected Kinship

As humanism in its development was becoming more and more materialistic, it also increasingly allowed its concepts to be used first by socialism and then by Communism. So that Karl Marx was able to say, in 1844, 'Communism is naturalised humanism'.

This statement has proved to be not entirely unreasonable. One does see the same stones in the foundations of an eroded humanism and of any type of socialism: boundless materialism; freedom from religion and religious responsibility (which under Communist regimes attain the stage of anti-religious dictatorship); concentration on social structures with an allegedly scientific approach. (This last is typical of both the Age of Enlightenment and of Marxism.) It is no accident that all of Communism's rhetorical vows revolve around Man (with a capital M) and his earthly happiness. At first glance it seems an ugly parallel: common traits in the thinking and way of life of today's West and today's East? But such is the logic of materialistic development.

The interrelationship is such, moreover, that the current of materialism which is farthest to the left, and is hence the most consistent, always proves to be stronger, more attractive and victorious. Humanism that has lost its Christian heritage cannot prevail in this competition. Thus, during the past centuries and especially in recent decades, as the process became more acute, the alignment of forces was as follows: liberalism was inevitably pushed aside by radicalism, radicalism had to surrender to socialism and socialism could not stand up to Communism. The Communist regime in the East could endure and grow due to the enthusiastic support from an enormous number of Western intellectuals who (feeling the kinship!) refused to see Communism's crimes, and when they no longer could refuse, they tried to justify these crimes. The problem persists: in our Eastern countries, Communism has suffered a complete ideological defeat, it is zero and less than zero. And yet Western intellectuals still look at it with considerable interest and empathy, and this is precisely what makes it so immensely difficult for the West to withstand the East.

Before the Turn

I am not examining the case of a disaster brought on by a world war and the changes which it would produce in society. But as long as we wake up every morning under a peaceful sun, we must lead an everyday life. Yet there is a disaster which is already very much with us. I am referring to the calamity of an autonomous, irreligious humanistic consciousness.

It has made man the measure of all things on earth – imperfect man who is never free of pride, self-interest, envy, vanity and dozens of other defects. We are now paying for the mistakes which had not been properly appraised at the beginning of the journey. On the way from the Renaissance to our days we have enriched our experience but we have lost the concept of a Supreme Complete Entity which used to restrain our passions and our irresponsibility. We have placed too much hope in political and social reforms, only to find out that we were being deprived of our most precious possession: our spiritual life. It is trampled by the Party mob in the East, by the commercial one in the West. This is the essence of the crisis: the split in the world is less terrifying than the similarity of the disease afflicting its main sections.

If, as claimed by humanism, man were born only to be happy, he would not be born to die. Since his body is doomed to death, his task on earth evidently must be more spiritual: not a total engrossment in everyday life, not the search for the best ways to obtain material goods and then their carefree consumption. It has to be the fulfilment of a permanent, earnest duty so that one's life journey may become above all an experience of moral growth: to leave life a better human being than one started it. It is imperative to reappraise the scale of the usual human values;

its present incorrectness is astounding. It is not possible that assessment of the President's performance should be reduced to the question of how much money one makes or to the availability of gasoline. Only by the voluntary nurturing in ourselves of freely chosen and serene self-restraint can mankind rise above the world stream of materialism.

Even if we are spared destruction by war, life will have to change in order not to perish on its own. We cannot avoid reassessing the fundamental definitions of human life and human society. Is it true that man is above everything? Is there no Superior Spirit above him? Is it right that man's life and society's activities should be ruled by material expansion above all? Is it permissible to promote such expansion to the detriment of our integral spiritual life?

If the world has not approached its end, it has reached a major watershed in history, equal in importance to the turn from the Middle Ages to the Renaissance. It will demand from us a spiritual blaze, we shall have to rise to a new height of vision, to a new level of life where our physical nature will not be cursed as in the Middle Ages, but, even more importantly, our spiritual being will not be trampled upon as in the modern era.

This ascension will be similar to climbing on to the next anthropologic stage. No one on earth has any other way left but – upward.